VOLUME NINETEEN

Book One
RESEARCH GAPS IN ALLIANCE DYNAMICS
Michael Don Ward

Book Two
TROJAN PEACE:
SOME DETERRENCE PROPOSITIONS TESTED
Theresa C. Smith

Book Three
THE LOGICAL CONSISTENCY AND SOUNDNESS
OF THE BALANCE OF POWER THEORY
Roslyn Simowitz

Book Four
INTERNATIONAL POLICY COORDINATION:
ISSUES IN OPEC AND EACM
Martin W. Sampson III

THE LOGICAL CONSISTENCY AND SOUNDNESS OF THE BALANCE OF POWER THEORY

Roslyn L. Simowitz

Volume 19
Book 3

MONOGRAPH SERIES IN WORLD AFFAIRS

Graduate School of International Studies
University of Denver
Denver, Colorado 80208

Library of Congress Cataloging in Publication Data

Simowitz, Roslyn L., 1950-
   The logical consistency and soundness of the balance of power theory.

   (Monograph series in world affairs, ISSN 0077-0582; v. 19, bk. 3)
   Bibliography: p.
   1. Balance of power—Mathematical models. I. Title. II. Series.
JX1318.S56   1983   327.1'12   82-21030
ISBN 0-87940-070-6

ABOUT THE AUTHOR

ROSLYN SIMOWITZ is an Assistant Professor of Political Science at Texas Tech University. She is currently a visiting scholar at the Institute for Latin American Studies, University of Texas at Austin, where she is researching bias in the reporting of foreign news. Her articles appear in *Teaching Political Science* and *Peace Research Society Papers (International)*.

790076

To the memory of John V. Gillespie,
to T. Eddie Bullard
and to
Barry L. Price

TABLE OF CONTENTS

The Logical Consistency and Soundness
of the
Balance of Power Theory

1

INTRODUCTION

The balance of power theory has been used by numerous historians, political scientists and statesmen to explain significant aspects of international behavior for much of the seventeenth, eighteenth, nineteenth and twentieth centuries. In recent times this theoretical perspective has strongly influenced the professional and political activities of key political figures such as Henry Kissinger and Zbigniew Brzezinski, two of the most prominent statesmen in contemporary American society. Scholars have used the theory to comprehend international behavior, while politicians have used it as a guide to rational decision-making in foreign affairs. The balance of power theory has been used to explain and predict a variety of consequences including the distribution of power between opposing alliances, the occurrence of war, and the survival of independent nations. Many writers also regard literature on deterrence and balance of terror to be outgrowths of this theory. The fact that the theory has been applied so frequently led Claude (1967:12) to remark that "'balance of power' is to international relations writers as 'a pinch of salt' is to cooks, 'stellar southpaw' to baseball writers, and 'dialectical materialism' to Marxist theoreticians."

Despite the significance of balance of power theory in the study of international politics, conflicting claims regarding the theory's consequences exist. Most writers agree that the resulting power distribution between competing actors is a major consequence, but they do not agree on what that distribution is. Schwarzenberger (1941:117-18) claims, for example, that "the grouping of nations into alliances and counteralliances produced an equal distribution of power between these forces" and describes the resulting power distribution as "an historical truism." Another writer claims, however, that

> if we look at the whole sweep of history for the past 150 years, we find that equal power distributions are the exception, not the rule ... a more accurate view of the distribution of power in the years 1815-1914 finds England the senior partner in a combination of overwhelming power (Organski, 1958:291-93).

3

In addition to conflicting claims concerning the resulting power distribution, there are contradictory arguments concerning the relationship between the power distribution and occurrence of war. One scholar, for example, believes that the existence of an equal power distribution between competing actors "tends to promote peace" (Claude, 1967:155), while another claims that "the periods of balance, real or imagined, are periods of warfare, while the periods of known preponderance are periods of peace" (Organski, 1958:292).

In light of the significance of this theory both as a guide to foreign policy-making and the analysis of international behavior, it is important that these contradictions be resolved. My study deals with them in a unique way, by examining three logical properties of the theory: consistency, soundness and applicability. Each property may account for the contradictions and each may serve as a criterion for eliminating them.

An analysis of consistency, soundness and applicability requires a precise statement of the theory's basic assumptions and conclusions. To date, however, there is no such statement in the literature. As a result, I reviewed the traditional literature on balance of power in order to abstract from it the theory's assumptions and conclusions. To facilitate the analysis, these assumptions or axioms are restated in mathematical form. When the axioms are represented in this way it is easier to trace their logical implications, which in turn helps to delimit the conditions for applicability and determine the theory's consistency and soundness.

The superiority of the axiomatic approach is due in large part to the fact that precision in verbally articulated theories is quite poor. Many statements appear contradictory because they are not properly qualified, and the task of qualifying them is made more difficult when they are left in their verbal form. An axiomatic approach, had it been adopted by writers in presenting this theory, would have facilitated an identification of those conditions subject to variation so that the apparently contradictory statements were seen to be compatible under different sets of conditions.

The axiomatic approach also simplifies identification of a theory's axioms and consequences. Although there is general agreement among writers in the literature concerning the consequences and axioms of the balance of power theory, at times axioms identified by one writer are identified as consequences by another.

Not only does an axiomatic approach aid in identifying the explicit axioms or assumptions of a theory, it also facilitates an identification of the theory's implicit assumptions. For example, one of the implicit assumptions in the balance of power theory is that alliances are the only means by which nations can change the power distribution in the system. For most

4

verbally articulated theories, it is difficult enough to distinguish between the explicit assumptions and consequences of the theory, but it is even more difficult to identify the theory's implicit assumptions. Had an axiomatic approach been used in presenting this and other verbally articulated theories, both the explicit assumptions and the underlying or implicit assumptions would have been more discernible.

The task of making valid arguments is facilitated and more amenable to verification once the theory is presented in axiomatic form. Stating theories in this way also furthers the objective to provide sound theories of political phenomena. Deriving sound or valid conclusions is more difficult if the assumptions of the theory are presented only verbally. In fact, the conclusions of many verbally articulated theories are not related to the theory's assumptions through a chain of deductive reasoning, but rather through a chain of additional assumptions. In this study, for example, the consequences concerning war and national survival are implied by the axioms through the use of additional assumptions. Efforts to provide theories capable of explaining and predicting political phenomena would be closer to realization if scholars adopted an axiomatic approach in articulating their theories.

LITERATURE REVIEW

Before elaborating on my efforts, it is desirable to review the attempts others have made to resolve the contradictions in the balance of power theory. A.F.K. Organski (1958) was probably the first scholar to confront this problem, by demonstrating that one of the conflicting claims was not valid. According to Organski, one of the theory's assumptions required uncommitted nations to ally with weaker nations or alliances threatened by more powerful opponents. Another assumption required uncommitted nations to pursue policies aimed at equalizing the power distribution of the two opponents. Organski reasoned that an equal power distribution between the two antagonists could not be produced if a very powerful nation attempted to equalize the power of the two opponents. He argued that if the nation which attempted to produce an equal distribution of power was a major nation, "the result should be a great preponderance of power on its side . . . the very thing it is designed to prevent" (Organski, 1958:286). Consequently, Organski claimed that the theory should not result in equal power distributions between two opposing actors; the claims of those who argued that it would be equal were therefore not valid.

Although Organski's argument is convincing, it is incomplete because it describes only one of several possible situations, in which the power of the uncommitted nation is greater than the difference in power between the opponents. Suppose the power of the uncommitted nation is equal to the difference in power between the two antagonists? If the uncommitted nation attempts to equalize the power of the two opponents, as Organski assumes, this situation results in an equal distribution of power between the two opponents. Here, the claims of those asserting that an equal distribution of power is produced are valid. Consequently, the apparently contradictory claims concerning the resulting power distribution are not resolved by Organski's treatment of the problem.

In another effort Singer, Bremer and Stuckey (1972) collected and analyzed data for the period 1870-1965 to examine the relationship between power distribution and the occurrence of war. Their results indicate that a relationship existed between peace and an equal distribution of power between actors in the nineteenth century, while a relationship existed between peace and an unequal distribution of power in the twentieth century, suggesting that the relationship between power distribution and war is different for different periods of time. But the authors do not attempt to explain what characteristics of each period could account for this. If two distinctive sets of assumptions were provided by balance of power theorists to reflect the characteristics of each of the two centuries, then we would know why one type of power distribution is related to war in one century but to peace in the other century. Obviously, distinctive sets of assumptions entail different and perhaps incompatible conclusions. But the authors who assert these contradictory claims do not provide a different set of assumptions for each century and neither do Singer, Bremer and Stuckey. As a result, we are unable to explain why one type of power distribution is associated with war in one century but with peace in the other century.

Another study dealing with contradictions in the literature was done by Riker (1962:159-87), who was interested in examining the stability of alliances in a balance of power system. Through his analysis he reached some conclusions regarding the theory's consistency. An inconsistent theory contains assumptions that imply contradictory conclusions. Hence, if the assumptions of the balance of power theory were found to be inconsistent, then the contradictory claims concerning its conclusions could be explained. Even though Riker's analysis was not primarily concerned with resolving the contradictions, it could be useful to explain how these conflicting claims came about.

Riker argued that the theory was inconsistent. To demonstrate this, he claimed that the following statements represented the assumptions of the balance of power theory:

1. All nations attempt to maximize their own power at each other's expense;
2. Dominant alliances are prevented from emerging in the system;
3. Nations ally with weaker nations or alliances that are threatened by more powerful ones.

According to Riker, the first assumption reflected the rationality of actors in a balance of power system, while the two remaining assumptions reflected the core features of the balance of power theory. He then asserted that the rationality assumption made by writers on balance of power was equivalent to the rationality assumption made in n-person, zero-sum games. An n-person, zero-sum game is one in which the sum of the gains and losses over all players equals zero. Riker used n-person, zero-sum game theory to predict which alliances formed. He found that minimal winning alliances formed. This result obviously violated assumption (2) because the minimal winning alliances that formed were also dominant alliances. Moreover, some of the minimal winning alliances that arose were the result of previously uncommitted nations that had subsequently allied with the stronger opponent. Consequently, Riker concluded that the balance of power theory was inconsistent because assumption (3) of the theory was also violated.

Unfortunately, there are several problems with Riker's analysis. As I mentioned above, Riker assumed that the assumption made regarding the rationality of actors in n-person, zero-sum games was equivalent to the rationality assumption made about actors in a balance of power system. Zinnes (1970: 351-62) however, has convincingly argued that the rationality assumption made in the context of n-person, zero-sum games is not equivalent to the rationality assumption made by writers who describe objectives of nations in a balance of power system, because in most cases balance of power systems cannot be characterized as zero-sum; nations could maximize their power without conflicting with other nations. Moreover, those balance of power systems that could be considered zero-sum situations did not involve all n-participants. In short, the assumptions Riker used to prove that alliances formed in violation of assumptions (2) and (3) of the theory were inappropriate.

Another problem with Riker's study was his description of the theory's assumptions. Assumption (1) asserts that all nations in the system attempt to maximize their power. Not all writers, however, describe the objective of nations to be power maximization. Many assume that in a balance of power system nations pursue policies aimed at equalizing the power between the opponents (Wright, 1942:748; Kissinger, 1957; Gulick, 1955; Morgenthau, 1956:13-19). Hence Riker's analysis is limited in its conclusion regarding the theory's consistency because it considers only one of several types of national policy objectives described in the balance of power literature. Once we assume that nations pursue other types of policy objectives, results inconsistent with the theory's remaining axioms may not occur. If so, the theory would be consistent, and contradictory claims in the balance of power literature would not be explained by the theory's inconsistency. Because of these problems, we must regard Riker's analysis of the balance of power theory's consistency as suspect and incapable of providing a comprehensive explanation of contradictions in the literature.

Briefly then, we have a theory which purports to explain significant aspects of international behavior, including the occurrence of war and the survival of independent nations. The literature in international politics attests to the importance and impact of this theory. But at the same time, the descriptions of this theory are replete with contradictory claims. This research attempts to extend efforts made earlier in resolving these conflicting claims. To do this, three properties of the balance of power theory are examined—consistency, soundness and applicability.

DEFINITIONS

Consistency

A theory is consistent if its axioms (or assumptions) do not imply contradictory statements. In other words, if it is possible to derive both Z and not Z (i.e., -Z) from the axioms of the theory, we can conclude that the theory is inconsistent. The symbol Z may refer to any propositional statement. For example, suppose that Z refers to the following:

Example 1.

Z: An equal distribution of power results between competing actors.

-Z: An unequal distribution of power results between competing actors.

Further suppose that the balance of power theory has two axioms, X and Y. In our example, they refer to the following:

X: All nations in the system attempt to maximize their power.

Y: All nations attempt to prevent the emergence of dominant actors.

Some people claim that X and Y imply Z while others claim that X and Y imply -Z. If we can show that X and Y imply both Z and -Z, then we will have demonstrated that this theory is inconsistent. This implication can be represented as the conditional statement:

$$X \& Y \rightarrow Z \& -Z.$$

8

If the axioms of the balance of power theory are inconsistent, we can conclude that they are responsible for the contradictory claims concerning the theory's consequences. If so, we are left with a theory that is incapable of explanation and prediction. If a theory's consequences are logically implied by its axioms, then these axioms provide an explanation for the theory's consequences. In our example, if X & Y → Z & -Z, then X & Y explain both Z and -Z. How can we be satisfied with an explanation of Z that also explains -Z? Furthermore, how useful are axioms X & Y when they predict both Z and - Z?

To recapitulate, if our study indicates that the axioms of the balance of power theory are inconsistent, we have an explanation for the contradictory claims concerning the theory's consequences. If the consequences are found to be inconsistent, we, of course, have a theory with limited utility for explanation, prediction and understanding. But in the process of demonstrating that the axioms of the theory are inconsistent, those axioms responsible for the contradictory statements will be identified. We will then be able to eliminate one of the axioms from the theory, thereby providing a consistent set of axioms.

At this point, however, we have only considered the possibility that the axioms are inconsistent. What if we find that they are consistent? Before we answer this question, we need to discuss the test used to determine if a theory is consistent.

One means of demonstrating that a theory is consistent is by deriving all of its logical implications to see if the axioms do not imply contradictory statements. If we cannot show that Z and -Z are both implied by the axioms, however, we cannot conclude that the theory is consistent, because it is impossible to know if and when we have specified all possible consequences of the theory's axioms. We cannot be sure, therefore, that both Z and -Z are not included in the set of all possible consequences. However, if we can demonstrate that some condition (or value) exists under which all the axioms of the theory are simultaneously satisfied, then we can conclude that the theory is consistent (Wilder, 1952). Since it is impossible to make Z and -Z (logically) true at the same time, an identification of conditions under which two or more axioms can be satisfied proves that they are not inconsistent. Let me provide an example to illustrate this test for consistency. Suppose we have a theory that contains two axioms:

Example 2.

Axiom 1. $x = -y$

Axiom 2. $x = y$

To show that these axioms are consistent, we need to demonstrate that some value (or number) exists that satisfies both axioms (1) and (2). The number zero satisfies both axioms and hence they are consistent. Briefly then, to demonstrate that the balance of power theory is consistent, we need to show that some condition or value exists under which all the axioms of the theory are simultaneously satisfied.

Returning to balance of power, if we find a condition under which all axioms of this theory are simultaneously satisfied, we can conclude that the theory is logically consistent. If, for example, axioms X and Y in Example (1) represent all of the axioms of the balance of power theory and C_1 is a condition that simultaneously satisfies X and Y, we can conclude that the theory is logically consistent. If we find that the theory is consistent, we must turn to another property of the theory — soundness — to resolve contradictions concerning the theory's conclusions.

Soundness

All theories are made up of a series of arguments. The assumptions of the argument are axioms of the theory and the consequences of the argument are a subset of the consequences of the theory. An argument is sound or valid if its consequences are logically implied by its assumptions. If an argument is sound, its assumptions (or axioms) provide an explanation for the argument's consequence(s). On the other hand, if an argument is not sound, its axioms do not explain its reputed consequence(s).

Perhaps some examples would demonstrate the importance of this property. The following syllogism is an example of a sound argument.

Example 3.

Axiom 1. All men are mortal.

Axiom 2. Socrates is a man.

Consequence: Socrates is mortal.

The conclusion that Socrates is mortal is explained by axioms (1) and (2) because this argument is sound.

Example (4), on the other hand, is an example of an argument that is not sound.

Example 4.

Axiom 1. All people who smoke die of cancer.

Axiom 2. Joe smokes.

Consequence: Joe dies of a heart attack.

The conclusion that Joe dies of a heart attack is not implied by axioms (1) and (2), and therefore these axioms do not explain why Joe dies of a heart attack.

Let us turn to the balance of power example described earlier. Suppose we find that axioms X and Y are consistent under some condition, say C_1.

Then we know that the contradictory claims, Z and -Z, are not the result of the theory's axioms being inconsistent. Further suppose that we can show Z is logically implied by X and Y under condition C_1. That is, suppose we can prove the following:

Example 5.

X & Y & C_1 → Z

where

X: All nations in the system attempt to maximize their power.

Y: All nations attempt to prevent the emergence of dominant actors.

C_1: All nations have equal amounts of power.

Z: An equal power distribution results between competing actors.

Z is therefore a valid (i.e., sound) conclusion and X, Y and C_1 explain the occurrence of Z. Moreover, -Z cannot be logically implied by X & Y & C_1.

Is it possible to conclude, on the basis of the above analysis of soundness, that those who assert -Z have made an invalid claim? We cannot definitively draw this conclusion because they claim only that X and Y are satisfied. They say nothing regarding the conditions under which these axioms are satisfied and imply -Z. It is possible that under some other condition, say C_2, that X & Y & C_2 → -Z. We therefore need to investigate this possibility before concluding that one group has made a valid claim while the other group has not. To do this we turn to the third property of the theory—applicability.

Applicability

We know a theory's applicability when we have identified all the conditions under which the axioms of the theory are simultaneously satisfied. In other words, a theory's applicability is known once we have specified the complete set of conditions that allow the theory's axioms to hold. To illustrate:

Example 6.

If $x^2 + y^2 = 1$, the set of integers [x, y: (x=1, y=0), (x=0, y=1), (x=-1, y=0), (x=0, y=-1)] identifies this statement's applicability; it identifies all the values that satisfy $x^2 + y^2 = 1$.

Let us apply the balance of power model to Example 6. Suppose we find that the set $[C_1, C_2]$ contains all conditions that satisfy axioms X and Y. Further suppose that Z is logically implied by X & Y under condition C_1 and Z is also logically implied by X & Y under condition C_2. That is,

Example 7.

1. $X \& Y \& C_1 \to Z$

2. $X \& Y \& C_2 \to Z$

where

X: All nations in the system attempt to maximize their power.

Y: All nations attempt to prevent the emergence of dominant actors.

C_1: All nations have equal amounts of power.

C_2: At least one pair but not more than three pairs of nations have unequal amounts of power.

Z: An equal distribution of power results between competing actors.

If our analysis produces results equivalent to those in Example 7 above, we can conclude that those who claim -Z is implied by axioms X and Y are making an incorrect inference.

On the other hand, suppose we find that Z is implied by X & Y under C_1 and -Z is implied by X & Y under C_2. That is,

Example 8.

1. $X \& Y \& C_1 \to Z$

2. $X \& Y \& C_2 \to -Z$

where X, Y, C_1, C_2, Z have the same meanings as in Example 7. If we find that our analysis produces results equivalent to those in Example 8, then we can conclude that both Z and -Z are valid claims. We also have an explanation for Z and -Z in terms of axioms X and Y, and conditions C_1 and C_2. However, in order to provide this kind of explanation for the contradictions in the literature, we must first determine the theory's applicability. Until we specify all conditions that satisfy X and Y and derive their implications, we cannot fully explain the contradictory claims. We can only conclude that one of the conflicting claims is not sound if we have shown that the other claim is valid under all conditions that satisfy the theory's axioms. We must therefore specify the theory's applicability to see if either or both of the contradictory claims are valid.

Examining the consistency, soundness and applicability of balance of power theory may resolve the contradictions in the literature. Each property may account for these contradictions and serve as a criterion for eliminating them. Consistency—whether or not the theory's axioms imply contradictory conclusions—is the first property to be investigated. To demonstrate consistency, we must show that some condition exists under which all the axioms of the theory are simultaneously satisfied. If we find that the theory is inconsistent we can eliminate the axioms(s) responsible for the contradiction(s).

If the theory is consistent, however, the other two properties—applicability and soundness—will be examined. To specify applicability, we must identify the entire set of conditions that satisfy the theory's axioms. To check for soundness, we must determine whether the consequences claimed for the theory are logically implied by the theory's axioms. An analysis of applicability must be done prior to the examination of soundness. Once the theory's applicability is known, we can determine whether each of the contradictory claims is sound under different sets of conditions, or whether one claim is sound while the other is not. If we find that one claim is sound while its contradiction is not, we reject the latter claim. By examining these three properties of the theory, we hope to resolve the contradictory assertions found in the literature.

While the notions of consistency, soundness and applicability are useful tools for resolving the contradictions in balance of power theory, they are also important in their own right. It is necessary, in fact, to consider all three properties before subjecting a theory to empirical analysis. If the axioms of a theory are inconsistent, then even if one of its consequences is supported by a data analysis, the theory cannot be used to explain or predict this consequence. An inconsistent theory explains and predicts in the most trivial and meaningless way because it can imply anything (i.e., Z and –Z). Similarly, if the axioms of a theory do not logically imply the reputed consequence, the theory neither explains nor predicts this consequence. On the other hand, if a data analysis does not support one of the theory's consequences, and the applicability of the theory is not identified prior to the data analysis, we cannot reject this theory. If we have not identified the conditions that satisfy the axioms and consequences of the theory, it is possible that the empirical test includes conditions that do not satisfy this consequence of the theory. It is conceivable, then, that a theory is not being accurately evaluated if one of its consequences is subjected to a data analysis before the applicability of the theory is specified.

An examination of these properties should not only precede the empirical analysis of a theory, but should also be used jointly with the empirical analysis in evaluating the utility of a theory. It is not uncommon for writers to choose between two or more competing explanations by subjecting the consequences implied by these theories to empirical analyses (Collier & Messick, 1975; Ostrom, 1977). When the researcher finds that the data fits one theory better than another, he or she often concludes that the theory with the higher correlation coefficient, in fact, provides a better explanation of the phenomena in question. But this data analysis is done prior to any analysis of the theory's consistency, soundness and applicability. That is, there is no prior determination of whether the consequences are logically implied by the axioms of the theory, whether the axioms are consistent, and under what conditions the theory is applicable. If the axioms of the theory with the poorer fit are consistent while the axioms of the theory with the better fit are inconsistent, then the researcher should conclude that the theory with the poorer fit provides a better explanation of the phenomena in question. Additionally, if the consequences of the theory with the better fit are not logically implied by the axioms, then this theory does not provide an explanation of the phenomena. Furthermore, if the conditions for applicability are not specified prior to the data analysis, then the poor fit of one of the theories may result from the fact that its consequence was not applicable under the tested conditions. In short, without first considering these logical properties, empirical tests are not only premature, they do not constitute a sufficient criterion for choosing between two or more competing explanations. The properties of consistency and soundness should be used to supplement the criterion of data analysis when choosing between competing theoretical explanations.

AN AXIOMATIC APPROACH

As noted, it is necessary to have an exact statement of the axioms and consequences in order to analyze a theory's consistency, soundness and applicability. To date, there is no precise statement of the balance of power theory's axioms and consequences. We need to review this literature in order to delineate these aspects of the theory.

Axioms and consequences abstracted from the general balance of power literature are described in detail later. Here, I will outline some major features of the theory. As shown in chapter 2, the first two axioms of the theory represent general areas of consensus among balance of power theorists. However, there is considerable disagreement involving the theory's remaining axioms. These involve policy objectives adopted by the nations and alliances in the system. Three different sets of axioms involving policy objectives are identified. The disagreement concerning these axioms is acknowledged by examining the consistency, soundness and applicability of each set of policy objectives together with the theory's first two axioms. That is, the first two axioms of the theory and each set of axioms describing policy objectives comprise a separate version of the theory and are therefore examined separately with regard to their consistency, soundness and applicability.

A review of the literature in chapter 5 also indicates that at least three consequences are claimed for the theory. While most writers agree that the resulting power distribution between competing actors is a major consequence, they do not agree on what that distribution is. Similarly, while writers agree that the occurrence of war is a major consequence of the theory, they do not agree on what power distribution leads to war. The only consequence on which little disagreement exists is that involving the survival of independent nations. Most writers agree that the balance of power theory has safeguarded the independence of nations in the system.

Although many contradictory claims in the literature concern the theory's consequences, there are also differences of opinion regarding the theory's applicability. Some writers, for example, claim that as the number of nations of comparable strength *increases*, the applicability of the theory increases. Others argue that as the number of nations of comparable strength *decreases*, the applicability of the theory increases. An axiomatic approach will enable me to examine these and other conflicting claims made with regard to the balance of power theory.

Chapter 2 of this study provides the foundation for the analysis; the axioms of the theory are abstracted from the literature and restated in mathematical form. Chapters 3 and 4 examine the consistency and applicability of the theory when the initial power distribution among nations is unequal. In chapter 5 the consequences of the theory are distilled from the literature and the soundness of the theory is examined. Chapter 6 examines the consistency, soundness and applicability when the initial power distribution among nations is equal. Chapter 7 summarizes the study.

2

AXIOMS OF BALANCE OF POWER THEORY

The first step in the analysis of consistency and applicability of the balance of power theory is establishing the theory's basic axioms. Since it is not a formal theory, these axioms must be drawn out of the traditional literature. There is considerable consensus regarding two of the theory's basic axioms—the absence of a dominant actor in the system, and the requirement that neutral nations ally with weaker actors (nations or alliances) that are threatened by more powerful actors pursuing hegemonic policies. Because there is consensus on these two, I refer to them as the *fixed axioms* of the theory.

Unfortunately, there is much less consensus regarding the remaining axioms. There is, for example, disagreement concerning the policy objectives of actors in the system. At least three versions of the theory are presented. All three contain the two fixed axioms but differ in their assumptions about the actors' policy objectives. The two fixed axioms are described first; then the different versions of the theory are presented.

Axiom 1: Distribution of Power in the System

The international system is described as one in which there is no nation or alliance whose power is greater than the total power of the system's remaining actors. For example, Vattel (1916) describes the balance of power as a system in which the *distribution of power* is such that "no state shall be in a position to have absolute mastery and dominance over the others." Pollard (1923:58) describes the *distribution of power* in the system as one in which there "is no need of strict equality and no necessary disturbance if one state grows stronger than another so long as the growth is not so great as to threaten the united strength of the others." And, in an analysis of numerous formulations of the theory, Kaeber (1906:22-25) finds the balance of power theory to imply "such a *distribution of power* in a multistate system such that no single state would be able, with impunity, to overawe the other states." In an extensive review of the balance of power literature, Zinnes (1967:272-73) finds "almost complete agreement on the

17

defining characteristics of a balance of power system . . . that a 'balance of power' involves a particular *distribution of power* among the states of the system so that no single state and no existing alliance has an 'overwhelming' or 'preponderant' amount of power." She provides the following generalization of the power distribution in the system:

$$"X_i < \sum_{i \neq j}^{n} X_j \text{ for } j = 1, \ldots n$$

where n = total number of nations in the system and X_i = power of the ith nation in the system." More recently Chatterjee (1972:55-56) argues that "the idea of no predominance is the essential analytic core of the classical balance of power theories; in spite of all the manifold variations with regard to description and application, this is one enduring feature generic to the concept itself." In constructing his formal model of the balance of power system, Chatterjee proposes the following axiom to describe the lack of dominance in the system: "of the set Q of coalitions, there is no dominant coalition. That is, for every S_i in Q_i,

$$k(S_i) \leqslant \sum_{i \neq j} k(S_j)$$

[where $k(S_i)$ is defined as the capabilities of coalition S_i and where Q_i is a partition of the set of national actors into disjoint coalitions] ."

The balance of power system may thus be seen to encompass any distribution of power so long as there is no one actor in the system whose power is greater than that of the remaining actors in the system. Clearly, Zinnes and Chatterjee provide the most precise formulations of this principle. Chatterjee's formalization is more general than Zinnes's in that it excludes from the set of all possible alliance structures those which include a dominant alliance. Obviously, one possible alliance structure is that in which all alliances are composed of single nations. When this is the case, Chatterjee's formulation is equivalent to Zinnes's. Since the literature contains references to dominant nations and alliances, Chatterjee's formulation of this principle is adopted as the first axiom of our model.

This axiom and the others to be presented are stated in terms of the notation given in Figure 1.

FIGURE 1

$A = [a_i, a_{-i}, \ldots a_n]$: set of nations in the system (It is assumed that there are n-nations in the system)

$A_j = [a_j, j \neq i, -i, j=1, \ldots m, m < n]$: set of neutral nations (A_j is a subset of A)

a_i, a_{-i} : opposing nations

$S_i, S_{-i}, \ldots S_j \ldots S_n$: nonoverlapping subsets of A ($S_i, \ldots S_n$ are the alliances in the system)

S_i, S_{-i} : opposing alliances

$U = [u_i, u_{-i} \ldots u_j \ldots u_n]$: preference functions (or utility functions which reflect ordinal preference patterns) of $a_i, a_{-i}, \ldots a_j \ldots a_n$ respectively

$K = [k_i, k_{-i}, \ldots k_j \ldots k_n]$: power of $a_i, a_{-i} \ldots a_j \ldots a_n$ respectively

$K(S_i)$: power of alliance S_i

$d = k_i - k_{-i}$: the difference in power of nations a_i and a_{-i}

$D = k(S_i) - k(S_{-i})$: The difference in power of alliances S_i and S_{-i}

$|d|$: the absolute value of the power difference of opposing nations

$|D|$: the absolute value of the power difference of opposing alliances

Definitions

Definition 1: An actor in the international system is a nation or an alliance.

Definition 2: Power is the ability of one actor (a_i, S_i) to get another actor (a_j, S_{-i}) to do something against its will. The sources of national power have traditionally been recognized as consisting of military and industrial capacities, population, geography and natural resources (Morgenthau, 1973: 106-24).

Definition 3: An independent nation is a nation that is sovereign within specified territorial boundaries (Morgenthau, 1973:302).

Definition 4: War is an act of organized violence between two or more actors (Morgan, 1977:27-28).

Definition 5: Peace simply means the absence of war.

Definition 6: An alliance exists if two or more nations with mutual interests pursue concerted policies or actions (Morgenthau, 1973:176).

Definition 7: $k(S_i) = \sum_{i \in S_i} k_i.$

The power of an alliance is the sum of the power of its members. Alliances are the major means of changing the distribution of power in a balance of power system. Once a nation becomes a member of an alliance, it substitutes the power of an alliance for its own power in calculating its relative power position in the system.

Definition 8: A dominant alliance is one in which $k(S_i) > \sum_{i \neq k} k(S_k)$.

A dominant alliance is one in which the power of one actor (nation or alliance) is greater than the summed total power of all other actors in the international system.

Definition 9: The major nations are those nations that place in the upper strata on such indicators of national power as military and industrial capacity, natural resources and population. The lesser nations, on the other hand, are nations that rank in the lower strata on most of these same indicators (Singer, et al., 1972:25-26).

Axioms

Axiom (1) can now be restated using Figure 1 and Definitions:

Axiom 1: For all S_i, S_k, $S_i \Omega S_k = \emptyset$, $k(S_i) \leqslant \sum_{i \neq k} k(S_k)$

This axiom says that there is no actor in the system whose power is greater than the summed total power of the remaining actors in the system.

Axiom 2: The Axiom of National Behavior

A second area of agreement among balance of power theorists concerns their claim that in a balance of power system, nations act to prevent the emergence of dominant actors with hegemonic ambitions. Sidney Fay (1937:395) describes the balance as "a 'just equilibrium' in power among the members of the family of nations as *will prevent* any one of them *from becoming* sufficiently strong to enforce its will upon the others." More recently, Kulski (1964:11-15) describes the balance of power as: " . . . a *maneuvering* among the three or several powers with one main objective in mind, *to prevent* any one of them from dominating the others." Penrose sees it as a system in which

> statesmen *must strive* [italics mine] to establish such relations with other countries as will ensure that no preponderance of power among the latter, singly or collectively, will threaten their independence or encompass their downfall. In the pursuit of this defensive aim they may decide from time to time, to enter into or form alliances with other powers. . . . (Penrose, 1965).

Kaplan (1957a:23) notes one of the essential rules of a balance of power system: "*Act to oppose* any coalition or single actor which tends to assume a position of predominance with respect to the rest of the system." As a guide to policy-making, Haas (1953a:371) describes the balance of power as a "system in which power was so distributed that no single state could acquire hegemony without *calling into existence* an alliance of all other states, an alliance strong enough to defeat the hegemony seeker." In his review of the literature, Claude finds frequent endorsement of this principle among balance of power theorists:

> When any state or bloc becomes, or threatens to become inordinately powerful, other states should recognize this as a threat to their security and *respond* [italics mine] by taking equivalent measures, individually, or jointly, to enhance their power. Within a balance of power system, this principle of equilibration has central importance as an operating rule (Claude, 1967:42-43).

Quite clearly, preventing the emergence of dominant actors appears as a description of national behavior. Nations enter into alliances to counteract the emergence of actors that pose a threat to others in the system. This constitutes the second axiom of our model.

Using Figure 1 and the following definition, this axiom is stated as:

21

Definition 10: a_i (or S_i) is said to pursue a hegemonic policy if a_i (S_i) seeks to maximize d (D).

where: $d = k_i - k_{-i}$ [and $D = k(S_i) - k(S_{-i})$] .

Axiom 2: If $k_i > k_{-i}$ [or $k(S_i) > k(S_{-i})$], and a_i (S_i) pursues a policy of hegemony, then a_j (a neutral nation) allies with a_{-i} (S_{-i}).

This axiom says that a neutral nation allies with an actor that is threatened by a more powerful one pursuing a hegemonic policy. Since the literature is ambiguous as to whether nations ally with actors threatened by *more powerful* ones (Kaplan 1957a:23) *or* whether nations ally with actors threatened by ones with *hegemonic ambitions* (Haas, 1953a:371), this axiom is represented in its weakest form; that is, it is violated only under a very restrictive set of conditions. The only violation of axiom (2) occurs when two actors are unequal in power, *and* the stronger actor pursues a hegemonic policy, *and* a neutral nation fails to ally with the weaker opponent.

According to axiom (2), a neutral nation allies with an actor that is threatened by a more powerful opponent with hegemonic ambitions. This axiom requires a system in which one nation or alliance threatens another nation or alliance. Without the condition of one actor (a_i or S_i) threatening another actor (the target, a_{-i} or S_{-i}), we cannot study the dynamics of the theory to see if and when the axioms are consistent and applicable. We therefore begin our analysis with the condition of one nation, a_i, threatening another nation, a_{-i} (the target nation), *either* by having *more power* than the target nation *or* by pursuing a *hegemonic policy* with respect to the target nation. These two nations, then, (the intimidating nation and the target nation) are the opposing nations. There are then only two opposing nations in the system. All other nations are initially neutral—they do not oppose each other and neither of the opposing nations threatens them. This condition guarantees maximum flexibility of alliance formations since all neutral nations are free to ally with either of the opposing nations. As a consequence, our analysis results in configurations of two opposing alliances and a number of neutral nations.

While this condition is somewhat limited, Morgenthau (1973:166-71) finds that "opposition of two alliances . . . is the most frequent configuration within the system of the balance of power." He describes the cases of "France and its allies opposing Russia in 1812, Japan opposing China from 1931 to 1941, the U.S. vs. the Axis from 1941 on," as situations which resulted in the opposition of two alliances. Waltz (1967:215-31) notes that "if balance of power politics is really played hard, it eventuates in two participants, whether states or groups of them." Kaplan (1957b:21-26) finds the history of the eighteenth and nineteenth centuries illustrative of two main antagonists which had their origins in one nation threatening the security of one or more nations. Healy and Stein (1971) discuss the applicability of the theory to the Franco-Prussian War where Germany and France were the two opposing nations and Austria, Russia and Britain were the neutral nations that allied with or opposed one of the two antagonists.

Of course, these remarks do not suggest how widespread this condition is in an overall historical sense. But they do suggest that it is fairly common within those periods typically characterized as balance of power epochs.

ADDITIONAL AXIOMS: EQUALITY OR HEGEMONIC POLICIES?

Axioms (1) and (2)—fixed axioms—represent areas of agreement in the general balance of power literature. There is no consensus, however, on the theory's remaining axioms which involve the policy objectives adopted by the actors in the system. Depending upon whether actors are motivated by a desire for power equal to or superior to that of their rivals, they pursue equality or hegemonic policies (known as balance of power policies). Three versions of the theory appear in the literature. In one version all nations in the international system pursue equality policies. In another, all nations pursue hegemonic policies. And in a third version, it is irrelevant which policies nations pursue as long as one nation in a balancer position pursues an equality policy. In each version writers assume that the theory is consistent, sound and applicable. The disagreement concerning national policy objectives is acknowledged, then, by examining the consistency, soundness and applicability of the theory when (a) all nations adopt policy objectives of equality, (b) all nations adopt hegemonic policy objectives, and (c) a nation in a balancer position adopts a policy objective of equality. That is, the implications of these different policy objectives are derived to determine when they are consistent with the fixed axioms of the theory.

Version 1: Balancer Version

According to the balancer version, applicability depends upon the existence of a balancer nation that pursues an equality policy and desires to produce an equal distribution of power between the system's opposing actors. Emphasis is placed on the final stage of alliance formation where all nations except the balancer are committed to one of two opposing alliances. If the balancer nation pursues an equality policy, it is believed that results consistent with axioms (1) and (2) are produced. Kulski, for example, writes that

> the system can best operate if all the great powers remain uncommitted and enjoy considerable latitude in their maneuvering to prevent the rise of one of them to a position of hegemony. But the *minimal condition is that at least one great power* of considerable strength *remain uncommitted* and the others be

kept in line by the potential sanction of its *throwing its weight on the scale of the weaker group against the stronger* [italics mine]. This power plays the role of the balancer, that is, of the state that keeps the balance in the distribution of power among the contending powers. As long as contending powers neutralize each other by their equal force, the balancer can stay aloof; if one of them or a group of them appears to overtake the rivals, the role of the balancer consists in stepping in diplomatically or even militarily, to restore the balance by adding its power to that of the weaker side (Kulski, 1964:12).

Similarly, Herz assumes that a necessary component is

the existence of one insular *power*, which, while geographically distant from the rest, would yet *intervene as "holder of the balance"* [italics mine] whenever the equilibrium [that is, an equal distribution of power] was endangered by the expansionist policies of a would be hegemony power (Herz, 1959:65).

According to Lerche, a balance of power system involves,

in addition to its ordinary members, a powerful nation standing in a peculiar relationship to the system — partly within the system, partly external to it — and able and willing to *"hold the balance"* [italics mine] by engaging in intricate maneuvers motivated by that purpose (Lerche, 1956).

The existence of a balancer nation pursuing an equality policy is viewed by these writers to be an essential component of the theory.

Writers who subscribe to the balancer version of the theory typically portray Great Britain in the balancer role. Hassell describes the British role during the eighteenth century in the following terms:

In 1717 Lord Stair, the English envoy, explained to the Regent that Stenhopes' foreign policy was based on the principle of a balance of forces; that it was England's objective to make Austria as far as possible equal in power to France, and to prevent either country from becoming superior in strength and influence to the other. And he stated frankly that if France endeavored to become more powerful than the Emperor she would lose her allies. . . . (Hassell, 1914:2-3).

Churchill's (1948:207-8) characterization of British foreign policy is similar to Hassell's. He writes that "for 400 years the foreign policy of England has been to oppose the strongest, most aggressive, most dominating power on the Continent, in joining the weaker states."

In the balancer version, writers assume there is one uncommitted (or neutral) nation left in the system, known as the balancer. All other nations are assumed to be allied with one of the two opposing actors. When the balancer nation pursues an equality policy objective, writers maintain that axioms (1) and (2) are simultaneously satisfied. That is, there is no dominant actor (nation or alliance) in the system and the balancer nation allies with the weaker of the two opponents.

Using Figure 1 and the following definitions, the equality policy of the system's remaining neutral nation (i.e., the balancer nation) and the equality and hegemonic policies of the two opposing alliances are stated below.

Definition 11: Two opposing actors (a_i and a_{-i}, or S_i and S_{-i}) are said to pursue equality policies if they attempt to minimize $|d|$, $|D|$ where $|d| = |k_i - k_{-i}|$ $|D| = |k(S_i) - k(S_{-i})|$.

Verbally, this means that opposing actors pursuing equality policies seek to minimize the difference in their power. In a balance of power system, opposing actors may minimize $|d|$, or $|D|$ by accepting other nations as allies.

Definition 12: Two opposing actors (a_i and a_{-i} or S_i and S_{-i}) are said to pursue hegemonic policies if:

a_i, S_i seek to maximize d, D respectively, where

$d = k_i - k_{-i}$ ($d \geqslant 0$) and $D = k(S_i) - k(S_{-i})$ ($D \geqslant 0$) and a_{-i}, S_{-i} seek to minimize $-d$, $-D$, respectively.

An opposing actor that pursues a policy of hegemony seeks to increase its power as much as possible vis-à-vis its opponent. In a balance of power system, opposing actors increase their relative power positions only by aligning with other nations.

Definition 13: A neutral nation, a_j, is said to pursue an equality policy if it seeks to minimize $|d|$ or $|D|$.

A neutral nation that pursues an equality policy attempts to minimize the difference in power between the system's opposing actors. In a balance of power system, a neutral nation pursuing an equality policy allies with an opposing actor if $|d|$ or $|D|$ decreases as a result.

Using Definitions (11), (12) and (13), the policy objectives of the actors in the balancer version of the theory follow.

Axiom (3) presents the preference function of an opposing actor that pursues a policy of equality.

Axiom 3:   *a.* If $|d|$, $|D|$ decrease, U_{S_i}, $U_{S_{-i}}$, u_i, u_{-i} increase.

         b. If $|d|$, $|D| = 0$, U_{S_i}, $U_{S_{-i}}$, u_i, u_{-i} are maximized.

         c. If $|d|$, $|D|$ increase, U_{S_i}, $U_{S_{-i}}$, u_i, u_{-i} decrease.

         [where $|d| = |k_i - k_{-i}|$ and $|D| = |k(S_i) - k(S_{-i})|$].

An opposing actor that pursues an equality policy seeks to minimize the power difference between itself and its opponent. In a balance of power system, an opposing actor accepts other nations as allies if $|d|$ or $|D|$ is reduced as a result. An opposing actor substitutes the power of the newly formed alliance for its own in calculating its relative power position.

Axiom (3') presents the preference function of an opposing actor that pursues a hegemonic policy.

Axiom 3': a. If D, d increase, U_{S_i}, u_i increase.

       b. If D, d decrease, U_{S_i}, u_i decrease.

       c. If D, d increase, $U_{S_{-i}}$, u_{-i} decrease.

       d. If D, d decrease, $U_{S_{-i}}$, u_{-i} increase.

       (where $d = (k_i - k_{-i})$ and $D = [k(S_i) - k(S_{-i})]$
       and $d \geqslant 0, D \geqslant 0$).

An opposing actor that pursues a hegemonic policy seeks to increase the power difference in its favor. In a balance of power system, an opposing actor increases the power difference in its favor by acquiring additional allies. An opposing actor substitutes the power of the newly formed alliance for its own in calculating its relative power position.

Axiom (4) describes the preference function of a neutral nation, a_j, that pursues an equality policy.

Axiom 4: a. If a_j allies with an opposing actor such that $|d|$, $|D|$ decreases, u_j increases.

      b. If a_j allies with an opposing actor such that $|d|$, $|D| = 0$, u_j is maximized.

      c. If a_j allies with an opposing actor such that $|d|$, $|D|$ increases, u_j decreases.

      [where $|d| = |k_i - k_{-i}|$ and $|D| = |k(S_i) - k(S_{-i})|$] .

This axiom says that if a neutral nation pursues an equality policy, its utility increases as the difference in power between the two opposing actors decreases. In a balance of power system a neutral nation pursuing an equality policy allies with the weaker of the two opponents if the difference in power between the opposing actors is thereby reduced. A neutral nation substitutes the power of the alliance for its own in calculating its relative power position in the system.

In the balancer version of the theory, it is assumed that alliance formation has progressed to the point where all nations are members of an opposing alliance except the "balancer nation." The two opposing alliances, S_i and S_{-i}, pursue either equality or hegemonic policies and the system's remaining neutral nation, a_j, pursues an equality policy. That is, the balancer nation acts in accordance with axiom (4) while S_i and S_{-i} act in accordance with axioms (3) or (3'). The consistency and applicability of this version of the theory is determined by varying the policy objectives of S_i and S_{-i} to see whether they produce results consistent with axioms (1), (2) and (4) (when one neutral nation acts in accordance with axiom [4]).

Version 2: Equality Version

According to the equality version of the theory, writers assume that all nations in the system pursue equality policies and are motivated by a desire to produce an equal distribution of power between the system's opposing actors.

Claude describes the equality version as one in which "the policies of most nations must be rationally directed toward the objective of equilibrium (that is, equality)." He further adds that

> this conception of the balance of power system contains the inherent recognition that if the process is to operate successfully, it must first be assumed that in any crisis precipitated by the ambition for preponderance of one state or combination of states, most other members of the system will be activated by the purpose of maintaining equilibrium (that is, equality) and will adopt rational and effective means to that end (1967:49-50).

Wright (1942:748) describes it as one in which "an objective for equality is adopted by all to preserve the balance of power system." von Gentz notes the role of

> appropriate alliances, dexterous negotiations, or (when necessary), force, in achieving the aim of organizing the federative constitution of Europe so skillfully that every weight in the political mass would find somewhere a counterweight (von Gentz, 1941:55).

Writers subscribing to the equality version of the theory assume that all nations in the system pursue equality policy objectives. When this is true, no dominant actor (nation or alliance) arises and nations ally with weaker actors that are threatened by more powerful ones.

The consistency and applicability of this version of the theory is examined by determining the conditions under which axioms (1) and (2) are consistent with axioms (3) and (4) when n-2 neutral nations act in accordance with axiom (4) and two opposing nations, a_i, a_{-i}, act in accordance with axiom (3). In other words, the mutual satisfiability of axioms (1), (2), (3) and (4) is determined when n-2 neutral nations have preference functions described by axiom (4) and two opposing nations have preference functions described by axiom (3).

Version 3: Hegemonic Version

In the hegemonic version, all nations in the system pursue hegemonic policies; all are assumed to be motivated by a desire to possess power superior to that of other actors in the system. When this is the case, it is assumed that axioms (1) and (2) are simultaneously satisfied.

Many writers describe the balance of power theory as one in which all nations pursue hegemonic policies. Kaplan (1957a:23), for example, describes the balance of power system as one in which "all nations act to increase their capabilities." He further claims that axioms (1) and (2) are satisfied by virtue of the fact that "even though a state desires to become preponderant itself, it must, to protect its own interest, act to prevent any other nation from accomplishing such an objective" (Kaplan, 1957b:690).

Charles Schleicher (1954:116) argues that "if each side emerges with relatively equal power, it is not because of policies directed toward that end, but it is rather the incidental outcome of ones intended to create a favorable margin of power." According to Claude,

> states need not be motivated to deliberately put power relations into equilibrium (that is, produce an equal distribution of power). The activating instinct may well be an urge to acquire more power than, not simply as much as, the competitors (Claude, 1967:47).

More recently, Hoffman (1972:620) describes the balance of power as a system in which "nations maximize their power at each others' expense." Spykman (1942:70) describes the nations in the system as "being interested in a balance which is in their favor, not an equal distribution of power, but a generous margin is their objective." In *Politics Among Nations*, Hans J. Morgenthau (1973:210) says ". . . all nations actively engaged in the struggle for power must actually aim not at a balance—that is, equality of power— but at superiority of power in their behalf." Arnold Wolfers (1962:81-85) describes the system as one in which the "efforts of all states are geared towards maximizing power."

All nations in the hegemonic version are motivated by the desire to secure more power for themselves vis-à-vis other actors in the system. By pursuing this objective, no dominant actors emerge and neutral nations ally with weaker actors threatened by more powerful opponents.

The hegemonic policy of opposing actors is described by axiom (3′) above. Opposing actors attempt to secure as much power for themselves vis-à-vis their opponent. According to axiom (3′), opposing actors increase the power difference in their favor by acquiring additional allies. Since every nation in the system is assumed to have some power, opposing actors are willing to accept *any nation* as an ally. They then substitute the power of the newly formed alliance for their own in calculating their relative power positions.

Neutral nations that pursue hegemonic policies may also increase their power by allying with other actors in the system. It is difficult, however, to determine the behavior of a neutral nation that pursues a hegemonic policy; it can choose to ally with *either opponent* in order to increase its relative power position.

Sociological theories of coalition formation in a triad suggest some interesting ways of conceptualizing the hegemonic policies of neutral nations. Some sociologists assume that coalition formation is to some extent dependent upon the external rewards to be obtained by a given coalition (Gamson, 1961; Riker, 1962; Chertkoff, 1967, 1970). However, balance of power theorists do not consider external rewards as a factor determining alliance formation. Rather, they argue that nations form alliances on the basis of their relative power positions and the overall distribution of power in the system. This is precisely what Caplow assumes in his particularly suggestive theory of coalition formation in a triad. Specifically, he assumes:

1. Members of a triad differ in strength; a stronger member can control a weaker member and will seek to do so.

2. Each member of the triad seeks control over the others. Control over one other is preferred to control over none. Additionally, control over one other is preferable to equality, and equality is preferable to being controlled by one other.

3. Strength is additive. The strength of a coalition is equal to the sum of the strengths of its members.

4. The formation of a coalition takes place in an existing triadic situation, so that there is a pre-coalition condition in every triad. Any attempt by a stronger member to coerce a weaker member will provoke the formation of a coalition to oppose the coercion (Caplow, 1956:489-93).

Caplow's assumptions are consistent with those of balance of power theorists who also infer from the power distribution and relative power position the action a neutral nation takes in pursuing a hegemonic policy (Wright, 1942:752-54; Rosecrance, 1963:28; Gulick, 1955:58-62). We therefore use Caplow's assumptions to define the hegemonic policies of neutral nations.

Definition 14: A *neutral nation*, a_j, is said to pursue a policy of hegemony if a_j seeks to increase its relative power position. a_j increases its relative power position by allying with other nations. As a member of an alliance, a_j substitutes the power of the alliance $[k(S_i)]$ for its own power (k_j) in determining its relative power position. Specifically, a_j increases its relative power position by allying with S_i if:

1. $k(S_i)_{a_j \epsilon S_i} > k(S_{-i})$ where, previously, $a_j \notin S_i$ and $k_j \leqslant k(S_{-i})$.

2. $k(S_i)_{a_j \epsilon S_i} = k(S_{-i})$ where, previously, $a_j \notin S_i$ and $k_j < k(S_{-i})$.

A neutral nation that pursues a hegemonic policy increases its power by increasing its relative power position with respect to other system members. For example, in a system where $k_j = k_i$ and $k_j > k_{-i}$, a_j prefers to ally with a_{-i} since it increases its relative power position with respect to a_i. By allying with other actors in the system, neutral nations may thereby increase their relative power positions.

Using Definition (14), the preference function of a neutral nation that pursues a hegemonic policy is stated in axiom (4').

Axiom (4') proposes a preference function for neutral nations that pursue hegemonic policies.

> *Axiom 4':* u_j increases if a_j's relative power position increases with respect to other actors in the system. Specifically, u_j increases if $a_j \epsilon S_i$ and:
>
> $a.$ $k(S_i)_{a_j \epsilon S_i} > k(S_{-i})$ where, previously, $a_j \notin S_i$ and $k_j \leqslant k(S_{-i})$.
>
> $b.$ $k(S_i)_{a_j \epsilon S_i} = k(S_i)$ where, previously, $a_j \notin S_i$ and $k(a_j) < k(S_{-i})$.

The consistency and applicability of the hegemonic version of the theory is analyzed by determining the mutual satisfiability of axioms (1), (2), (3') and (4') when two opposing nations, a_i and a_{-i}, act in accordance with axiom (3') and n-2 neutral nations act in accordance with axiom (4'). If there are any conditions under which these axioms are simultaneously satisfied, the hegemonic version is consistent. The applicability of the hegemonic version is determined by specifying the entire set of conditions under which these axioms are simultaneously satisfied.

To sum up, the balancer version of the theory contains two opposing alliances acting in accordance with axioms (3) or (3'), one neutral nation acting in accordance with axiom (4), and the two fixed axioms. The equality version contains two opposing nations acting in accordance with axiom (3), n-2 neutral nations acting in accordance with axiom (4), and the two fixed axioms. Finally, the hegemonic version contains two nations acting in accordance with axiom (3'), n-2 neutral nations acting in accordance with axiom (4') and the two fixed axioms. To analyze the theory's consistency, it is necessary to determine if any conditions exist under which these different combinations of policy objectives are consistent with the theory's fixed axioms. In analyzing the theory's applicability, it is necessary to determine the *entire* set of conditions under which the different combinations of policy objectives are consistent with the two fixed axioms.

AUXILIARY ASSUMPTIONS

Before proceeding to the analysis, two underlying assumptions, implicit in this analysis and referred to as auxiliary assumptions, must be discussed. The first says that the distribution of power in the system is altered only through the process of alliance formation, and is implicit in the balance of power literature. The second says that actors (nations and alliances) have perfect information regarding the power of all other actors in the system. Unlike the first assumption, this one is not implicit but is made with the intention of enhancing the theory's consistency and applicability. It is often argued that the lack of perfect information accounts for empirical inconsistencies of axioms (1) and (2). By making the assumption of perfect information, the theory's consistency and applicability should be enhanced.

Auxiliary Assumption 1: Changing the Power
Distribution Through Alliances

Implicit in the balance of power literature is the assumption that alliances are the only means by which nations can alter the distribution of power in the system; other means of enhancing national power have a negligible impact. Nations must form the appropriate alliances in pursuing their policy objectives. Organski (1958:302) describes the balance of power system as one in which "nations are fundamentally static units whose power is not changed from within," and states that the balance of power system is "maintained primarily by the skillful formation of alliances and counter-alliances." Gulick (1955:58-62) views alliances "as the primary means of altering the power distribution" and regards it as "the most prominent means of putting the balance of power theory to work." Claude characterizes the balance of power system as an "alliance system," and he provides the following rationale:

> States struggling for what they regard as appropriate places in the distribution of power discover readily enough that they can enhance their power not only by the "natural" method of building up their own resources, but also by an "artificial" method of linking themselves to the strength of other states. Indeed, this is the only method available to the bulk of states in the actual circumstances of modern history. Small states obviously cannot hope individually to balance, much less over-balance their great power neighbors: the only course open to them in the quest for security within a balance of power system is to seek a position in a grouping of states which considered as a collectivity, assumes the role of a major participant in the struggle for power (Claude, 1967:89).

Auxiliary Assumption 2: Perfect Information

This analysis assumes that actors in the system have perfect information regarding the power of all other systemic actors. Although writers assume that actors measured the power of other actors in the system, the inability to obtain accurate measurements of power is often cited as a major cause of the empirical violations of axioms (1) and (2). The purpose of this analysis is to determine the consistency and applicability of the theory when a condition cited as a major cause of the theory's inapplicability is eliminated.

Balance of power theorists assume that statesmen measured the power of other actors in the system. This assumption is implicit in the theory's axioms which describe the policy objectives of the system's actors. To pursue policies based on power considerations alone, it is assumed that statesmen measured the power of all the actors in the system. Haas finds that

> the overwhelming majority of analysts who have concentrated on the balance of power theory assume that the power position of the various states in the system is the only factor of importance which must guide statesmen in the decision making process (Haas, 1953a:378).

Wright claims that balance of power theorists assume

> that statesmen who pursue balance of power policies do so intelligently—they measure the factors involved in the balance of power accurately and guide their behavior by these calculations (Wright, 1942:753).

Rosecrance (1963:28) writes that "the balancing system of Europe required states to ally or oppose each other according to the presumed distribution of power." Implicit in this requirement is the assumption that nations attempted to determine the power of other actors in the system.

In fact, several citations in the literature attest to the fact that statesmen performed such calculations. Talleyrand, for example, urged Napoleon to adopt an equality policy in compensating Austria. "The proposed exchange of lands was worked out by the French minister in terms of population, territorial extent, and income, and an attempt was made to indicate the comparable value of each" (Bertrand, 1889:171). Again, during the Congress of Vienna, statesmen resorted to a similar system of measurement to determine the exchange and distribution of German and Polish territories to Prussia, Russia and Austria (Gulick, 1955:26). Wright argues that

> in spite of the difficulty, rough estimates (of power) were continually made. For instance, the great powers are compared to

the secondary power and to the small states, and the relative power of the seven great powers has sometimes been estimated: In 1922 the Washington arms conference rated the principal naval powers, Great Britain, the U.S., Japan, France, and Italy, respectively, at 5: 5: 3: 1.75: 1.75 (Wright, 1942:753).

The fact that it was basically impossible to make accurate measurements of power is often cited as a reason for the empirical violations of axioms (1) and/or (2) and the unsuccessful operation of a balance of power system. Gulick (1955:28) states that ". . . in actual fact, a singularly complex problem is presented by the measurement of power, and such measurement is not at all a trustworthy process, as it is assumed to be by balance of power theorists." Gulick further adds ". . . that statesmen could have made accurate power estimates was impossible, just as it is today. That they were compelled to rely on half-truths was one of the weaknesses of their system."

Kaplan (1957b:27-36) argues that "failures of information which prevent a national actor from taking the required measures to protect its own international position" are responsible for the violations of axioms (1) and (2) found in historical accounts. Morgenthau (1973:197-201) agrees that "the uncertainty of power calculations makes the balance of power incapable of practical application." Cobden asserts that the theory of the balance of power

> could be discarded as fallacious, since it gives no definition—whether by breadth, or territory, number of inhabitants, or extent of wealth—according to which in balancing the respective powers, each state shall be estimated (Cobden, 1867:269).

Apparently, the assumption that measurements of power were made is implicit (and sometimes explicit) in the balance of power literature. The fact that such measurements were often inaccurate is frequently cited as a cause of the empirical violations of axioms (1) and (2). In our model we assume that actors in the system have complete information regarding the power of all others. In making the assumption that actors have complete information, one of the causes for the empirical inconsistencies of axioms (1) and (2) is eliminated. It therefore becomes possible to determine if these axioms are theoretically consistent. This assumption then, enables us to determine whether having perfect information does in fact provide a consistent set of axioms when a condition that is cited as producing results inconsistent with axioms (1) and (2) is removed.

The following chapter examines the conditions under which the fixed axioms are consistent with the policy objectives of the balancer version of the theory.

3

CONSISTENCY AND APPLICABILITY OF
THE BALANCER VERSION

Aside from axiom (1), most writers do not place any restrictions on the initial distribution of power among nations in a balance of power system. That is, as long as no nation's power is greater than the summed power of the system's remaining actors, all types of initial power distributions are permissible. The following analysis examines the consistency and applicability of the balancer version of the theory when the initial power distribution is unequal. If the initial power distribution is unequal, there is at least one pair of nations, a_i, a_{-i}, such that $k_i > k_{-i}$, and

$$k_\ell \not> \sum_{\ell \neq k}^{n} k(S_k)$$

(in accordance with axiom [1]). The dyad, a_i, a_{-i}, are the system's opposing nations.

In the balancer version it is assumed that all nations except one have allied with either a_i or a_{-i} to form two opposing alliances, S_i and S_{-i}. The balancer version therefore contains three actors: S_i, S_{-i} and the balancer nation a_j. The two opposing alliances may pursue equality or hegemonic policies. Although most writers claim that the balancer nation pursues an equality policy, a few argue that the balancer nation pursues a hegemonic policy (Spykman, 1942:70; Nicholson, 1946:123; Organski, 1958:290-93). To determine the impact of the balancer nation's policy objective on the theory's applicability and consistency, we analyze the cases which arise when the balancer nation pursues an equality and a hegemonic policy. The analysis therefore involves three actors, S_i, S_{-i} and a_j, each pursuing equality or hegemonic policies. In order to examine the applicability and consistency of the balancer version, it is necessary to vary the policy objectives of the system's three actors, S_i, S_{-i} and a_j, to determine the conditions under which the different sets of policy objectives are consistent with the two fixed axioms.

Although it is assumed that the system contains a dyad such that $k_i > k_{-i}$, it is possible that the opposing alliances which form are equal or unequal in power. That is, either $k(S_i) = k(S_{-i})$ or $k(S_i) > k(S_{-i})$. When $k(S_i) = k(S_{-i})$ writers argue that the balancer nation remains neutral (in accordance with axiom [1]). On the other hand, when $k(S_i) > k(S_{-i})$, writers argue that the balancer nation allies with the weaker alliance (in accordance with axiom [2]). It is therefore necessary to vary the policy objectives of S_i, S_{-i} and a_j when (a) $k(S_i) = k(S_{-i})$ and (b) $k(S_i) > k(S_{-i})$ to see whether results consistent with axioms (1) and (2) are produced.

In order to analyze the consistency and applicability of the theory, it is necessary to consider the possible power relationships among the system's actors. The equality and hegemonic policies of opposing alliances and the equality policy of neutral nations (represented by axioms [3], [3'] and [4]) require knowledge of the relationship between the power of the balancer nation, and the difference in power between the system's opposing alliances. The power of the balancer nation, k_j, may be greater than, equal to, or less than the difference in power between the system's opposing alliances (i.e., $k_j \gtreqless D$). For each combination of policy objectives, $k_j \gtreqless D$ must be analyzed.

To determine the behavior of neutral nations pursuing hegemonic policies, additional information regarding the power relationships among the system's actors is necessary. Axiom (4'), which describes the hegemonic policy of neutral nations, requires knowledge of the relative power relationships between a_j and S_i and a_j and S_{-i}, k_j may be $\gtreqless k(S_i)$ and k_j may be $\gtreqless k(S_{-i})$. In addition to considering the relationship between k_j and D, it is also necessary to consider the cases generated by the possible power relationships between a_j and S_i and a_j and S_{-i}, in analyzing the cases when a_j pursues a hegemonic policy.

To sum up, the cases examined in analyzing the consistency and applicability of the balancer version are generated by varying the policy objectives of the system's actors, the relationship between k_j and D, and the relationship between k_j, $k(S_i)$ and $k(S_{-i})$ when the balancer nation pursues a hegemonic policy. (See Tables 1 and 2.)

Table 1 describes the cases analyzed when the distribution of power between the system's opposing alliances is equal. The analysis is considerably simplified when $k(S_i) = k(S_{-i})$. When the power of the system's opposing alliances is equal, $D = 0$ and it is therefore only necessary to consider $k_j > D$ for each set of policy objectives. Additionally, the analyses of cases 2 and 5 (where S_i pursues an equality policy and S_{-i} pursues a hegemonic policy) are equivalent to analyses of S_{-i} pursuing an equality policy and S_i pursuing a hegemonic policy since S_i and S_{-i} are indistinguishable when they have equal amounts of power. Finally, when a_j pursues a hegemonic policy, it is only necessary to consider the relationship between k_j and $k(S_i)$ because $k(S_i) = k(S_{-i})$.

When $k(S_i) > k(S_{-i})$, there are more cases to consider as Table 2 indicates. The analysis of $k(S_i) > k(S_{-i})$ is more involved than the analysis of $k(S_i) = k(S_{-i})$.

When $k(S_i) > k(S_{-i})$, $D > 0$ and it is necessary to consider $k_j \gtrless D$ for each combination of policy objectives. The analyses of cases 2 and 7 differ from the analyses of cases 3 and 6 in that the more powerful alliance pursues a hegemonic policy in cases 2 and 7 whereas the weaker alliance pursues a hegemonic policy in cases 3 and 6. Furthermore, when a_j pursues a hegemonic policy, it is necessary to consider the relationship between k_j and $k(S_i)$, and k_j and $k(S_{-i})$ since $k(S_i) \neq k(S_{-i})$.

CONSISTENCY AND APPLICABILITY OF THE BALANCER VERSION WHEN $k(S_i) = k(S_{-i})$

The cases listed in Table 1, when $k(S_i) = k(S_{-i})$, show that the balancer version of the theory is consistent if any conditions exist under which the axioms are simultaneously satisfied. The applicability of the theory is determined by specifying the entire set of conditions under which the axioms are simultaneously satisfied.

Assume: $k(S_i) = k(S_{-i})$. $D = 0$

Case 1. S_i and S_{-i} pursue *equality policies* and a_j pursues an *equality policy*. The theory is consistent if axioms (1), (2), (3) and (4) are simultaneously satisfied when S_i and S_{-i} act in accordance with axiom (3) and a_j acts in accordance with axiom (4).

According to axiom (4), the utility function of a_j is maximized when $|D| = 0$. Since $|D| = 0$, a_j's utility is maximized when a_j remains neutral. The utility functions of S_i and S_{-i} are maximized when $|D| = 0$ and they therefore do not want any additional allies. There is no dominant actor in the system [since $k(S_i) = k(S_{-i})$] and axiom (1) is therefore satisfied. Furthermore, no actor in the system is opposed by a more powerful actor with hegemonic ambitions and axiom (2) is satisfied.

The balancer version of the theory is therefore *consistent* since conditions exist under which axioms (1), (2), (3) and (4) are simultaneously satisfied. The analysis that follows proceeds to delineate the entire set of conditions under which the axioms of the balancer version are simultaneously satisfied.

Case 2. S_i pursues an *equality* policy (axiom [3]), S_{-i} pursues a *hegemonic* policy (axiom [3']) and a_j pursues a *hegemonic* policy (axiom [4']).

37

TABLE 1

CASES EXAMINED IN THE BALANCER VERSION
WHEN $k(S_i) = k(S_{-i})$

$k(S_i) = k(S_{-i})$
Case 1 S_i, S_{-i} and a_j pursue equality policies $k_j > D$
Case 2 S_{-i} and a_j pursue hegemonic policies and S_i pursues an equality policy $k_j > D$ $k_j \gtrless k(S_i) = k(S_{-i})$ (The analysis of this case is equivalent to the analysis of S_i pursuing a hegemonic policy and S_{-i} pursuing an equality policy.)
Case 3 S_i and S_{-i} pursue hegemonic policies and a_j pursues an equality policy $k_j > D$
Case 4 S_i and S_{-i} pursue equality policies and a_j pursues a hegemonic policy $k_j > D$ $k_j \gtrless k(S_i) = k(S_{-i})$
Case 5 S_i and a_j pursue equality policies and S_{-i} pursues a hegemonic policy $k_j > D$ (The analysis of this case is equivalent to the analysis of S_i pursuing a hegemonic policy and S_{-i} pursuing an equality policy.)
Case 6 S_i, S_{-i} and a_j pursue hegemonic policies $k_j > D$ $k_j \gtrless k(S_i) = k(S_{-i})$

TABLE 2

CASES EXAMINED IN BALANCER VERSION
WHEN $k(S_i) > k(S_{-i})$

$k(S_i) > k(S_{-i})$

Case 1	S_i, S_{-i} and a_j pursue equality policies $D \gtrless k_j$
Case 2	S_{-i} and a_j pursue equality policies, s_i pursues a hegemonic policy $D \gtrless k_j$
Case 3	S_i and a_j pursue equality policies, S_{-i} pursues a hegemonic policy $D \gtrless k_j$
Case 4	S_i and S_{-i} pursue equality policies, a_j pursues a hegemonic policy $D \gtrless k_j$, $\quad D > k_j \rightarrow k_j < k(S_i)$ & $k_j \gtrless k(S_{-i})$ $D = k_j \rightarrow k_j < k(S_i)$ & $k_j \gtrless k(S_{-i})$ $D < k_j \rightarrow k_j \gtrless k(S_i)$ & $k_j \gtrless k(S_{-i})$
Case 5	S_i and S_{-i} pursue hegemonic policies, a_j pursues an equality policy $\quad D \gtrless k_j$
Case 6	S_{-i} and a_j pursue hegemonic policies, S_i pursues an equality policy $D \gtrless k_j$, $\quad D > k_j \rightarrow k_j < k(S_i)$ & $k_j \gtrless k(S_{-i})$ $D = k_j \rightarrow k_j < k(S_i)$ & $k_j \gtrless k(S_{-i})$ $D < k_j \rightarrow k_j \gtrless k(S_i)$ & $k_j \gtrless k(S_{-i})$
Case 7	S_i and a_j pursue hegemonic policies, S_{-i} pursues an equality policy $D \gtrless k_j$, $\quad D > k_j \rightarrow k_j < k(S_i)$ & $k_j \gtrless k(S_{-i})$ $D = k_j \rightarrow k_j < k(S_i)$ & $k_j \gtrless k(S_{-i})$ $D < k_j \rightarrow k_j \gtrless k(S_i)$ & $k_j \gtrless k(S_{-i})$
Case 8	S_i, S_{-i} and a_j pursue hegemonic policies $D \gtrless k_j$, $\quad D > k_j \rightarrow k_j < k(S_i)$ & $k_j \gtrless k(S_{-i})$ $D = k_j \rightarrow k_j < k(S_i)$ & $k_j \gtrless k(S_{-i})$ $D < k_j \rightarrow k_j \gtrless k(S_i)$ & $k_j \gtrless k(S_{-i})$

The theory is applicable if axioms (1), (2), (3), (3') and (4') are simultaneously satisfied.

The hegemonic policy of a_j (expressed by axiom [4']) requires knowledge of the power relationships between a_j, S_i and S_{-i}. Since $k(S_i) = k(S_{-i})$, the following possibilities exist: $k_j < k(S_i)$, $k_j = k(S_i)$ and $k_j > k(S_i)$.

2a. $k_j < k(S_i)$.

When $k_j < k(S_i)$, S_i and S_{-i} are more powerful than a_j. By condition *(a)* in axiom (4'), u_j increases if a_j allies with either S_i or S_{-i}. If a_j allies with either S_i or S_{-i}, a_j substitutes the power of the newly formed alliance for its own in calculating its relative power position. The alliance which a_j joins is now more powerful than its opponent. S_i, however, is not willing to admit a_j as a member since it pursues an equality policy (axiom [3]) and its utility is maximized. S_{-i}, on the other hand, is willing to admit a_j as a member since it pursues a hegemonic policy and its utility increases as the difference in power between S_i and S_{-i} increases in its favor. Therefore, a_j allies with S_{-i}. As a result of this alliance, *axiom (1) is not satisfied.* When a_j is a member of S_{-i}, $k(S_{-i})$ is greater than $k(S_i)$.

2b. $k_j = j(S_i) = k(S_{-i})$

According to *(b)* in axiom (4'), a_j prefers to ally with S_i or S_{-i}. If a_j remains neutral, a_j is not more powerful than any other actor in the system [since $k_j = k(S_i)$]. However, if a_j allies with either S_i or S_{-i}, a_j becomes more powerful than one of the system's actors since a_j substitutes the power of the newly formed alliance for its own in calculating its relative power position. Hence, a_j prefers to ally with either opponent and S_{-i} is willing to admit a_j as a member (by axiom [3']). *Axiom (1) is not satisfied.*

2c. $k_j > k(S_i) = k(S_{-i})$

In this case, a_j is more powerful than S_i and S_{-i}. According to (4'), a_j has no incentive to ally with either opponent because it cannot enhance its relative power position in the system. Consequently, a_j remains neutral and the *theory is applicable.*

To sum up, when S_{-i} and a_j pursue hegemonic policies, and S_i pursues an equality policy, the theory is applicable only if $k_j > k(S_i) = k(S_{-i})$. Because the logic is very similar in all six cases, four remaining cases are shown in Appendix A. However, Table 3 summarizes the conditions under which the balancer version is applicable when $k(S_i) = k(S_{-i})$. The existence of these conditions indicates that the balancer version is logically consistent. The right column of Table 3 shows that this version is logically consistent regardless of the policy objectives pursued by the actors (S_i, S_{-i} and a_j).

The applicability of this version is affected, however, by the policy objectives of S_i, S_{-i} and a_j and their relative power positions. That is, the extent to which the axioms of the theory are simultaneously satisfied depends upon the policy objectives that S_i, S_{-i} and a_j pursue and the power differences between S_i, S_{-i} and a_j. In cases 1, 3, 4 and 5 of Table 3, the range of applicability is most extensive since there are no restrictions on the power relations between S_i, S_{-i} and a_j. The majority of actors in cases 1, 4 and 5 pursue equality policies. In case 3, although the majority of actors (S_i and S_{-i}) pursue hegemonic policies, the applicability is as extensive as in cases 1, 4 and 5 because the balancer nation pursues an equality policy. However, when one of the alliances and the balancer nation pursue hegemonic policies (cases 2 and 6), the theory is less applicable. The right column of Table 3 for cases 2 and 6 indicates that there are restrictions regarding the permissible power relations between S_i, S_{-i} and a_j.

The balancer version, then, is logically consistent when the power of the opposing alliances is equal and its internal consistency is not contingent upon the policy objectives nor the power relations of the actors in the system. However, the applicability is affected by the power relations and policy objectives of the system's actors. As long as the majority of actors pursue equality policies *or* the balancer nation pursues an equality policy, there are no restrictions on the theory's applicability. But when one of the opposing alliances and the balancer nation pursue hegemonic policies, the range of applicability is more limited.

This portion has assumed that both alliances had equal amounts of power. However, it is also possible that opposing alliances can have unequal amounts of power. In fact, the balancer version is used most often to describe situations in which one alliance is more powerful than its opponent. To determine the applicability of the theory when $k(S_i) > k(S_{-i})$, the policy objectives of the three actors, S_i, S_{-i} and a_j are varied, and the possible relationships between k_j and D are considered ($k_j \lessgtr D$) for each combination of policy objectives. Additionally, the power relationships between a_j, S_i and a_j, S_{-i} are taken into consideration when a_j pursues a hegemonic policy. Conditions under which each set of policy objectives is consistent with the theory's fixed axioms follow.

APPLICABILITY OF THE BALANCER VERSION
WHEN $k(S_i) > k(S_{-i})$

Assume: $k(S_i) > k(S_{-i})$. $D > 0$.

Case 1. S_i, S_{-i} and a_j pursue *equality* policies. The theory is applicable if axioms (1), (2), (3) and (4) are simultaneously satisfied when S_i and S_{-i} act in accordance with axiom (3) and a_j acts in accordance with axiom (4).

1a. $k_j < D$.

Since a_j seeks to minimize $|D|$, a_j allies with S_{-i}. *Axiom (1)*, however, is *automatically violated* when $D > k_j$ since S_i is a dominant alliance whose

TABLE **3**

APPLICABILITY OF BALANCER VERSION
WHEN $k(S_i) = k(S_{-i})$

Case 1	S_i, S_{-i} and a_j pursue equality policies	Applicable
Case 2	S_{-i} and a_j pursue hegemonic policies S_i pursues an equality policy	Applicable only when $k_j > k(S_i) = k(S_{-i})$
Case 3	S_i, S_{-i} pursue hegemonic policies a_j pursues an equality policy	Applicable
Case 4	S_i, S_{-i} pursue equality policies a_j pursues a hegemonic policy	Applicable
Case 5	S_i, a_j pursue equality policies S_{-i} pursues a hegemonic policy	Applicable
Case 6	S_i, S_{-i}, and a_j pursue hegemonic policies	Applicable only when $k_j > k(S_i) = k(S_{-i})$

42

power is greater than the total power of the remaining actors (i.e., S_{-i}, $a_j \epsilon S_{-i}$) in the system. It is therefore unnecessary to consider the possibility of $k_j < D$ in the remainder of the analysis.

   1b. $D = k_j$.

In this case a_j allies with S_{-i} and D is equal to zero. $k(S_i) = k(S_{-i})$ ($a_j \epsilon S_{-i}$) and the *theory is applicable.*

   1c. $D < k_j$

a_j seeks to minimize $|D|$ according to axiom (4). When the difference in power between S_i and S_{-i} decreases, the utility function of a_j increases. Thus if

   1c.1. $[k_j + k(S_{-i})] - k(S_i) < k(S_i) - k(S_{-i})$,

the utility function of a_j increases and a_j allies with S_{-i}. The inequality in 1c.1 may be simplified to: $k_j < 2D$. If condition 1c.1 is satisfied, the theory is inapplicable. Now S_{-i} (with $a_j \epsilon S_{-i}$) is a dominant alliance whose power is greater than S_i, thereby *not satisfying axiom (1).*

On the other hand, if

   1c.2. $[k_j + k(S_{-i})] - k(S_i) \geqslant k(S_i) - k(S_{-i})$,

a_j remains neutral since $|D|$ increases if a_j joins S_{-i}. This expression may be simplified to $k_j \geqslant 2D$. If the inequality in 1c.2 holds, the *theory is applicable.* As a result of a_j remaining neutral, there is no dominant actor in the system whose power is greater than the total power of the other actors. (That is, axiom [1] is satisfied.)

Although S_i opposes S_{-i} by having more power than S_{-i}, axiom (2) is not satisfied only if S_i is more powerful than S_{-i} *and* S_i pursues a hegemonic policy with respect to S_{-i}, *and* a_j does not ally with S_{-i}. In this case, S_i is more powerful than S_{-i} and a_j does not ally with S_{-i}, but S_i does not pursue a hegemonic policy with respect to S_{-i}. Therefore, axiom (2) is also satisfied and the theory is applicable.

Perhaps some numerical examples may help to clarify the analysis of cases *1c.1* and *1c.2*. When a_j pursues an equality policy it wants to minimize $|D| = |k(S_i) - k(S_{-i})|$. If the power of S_i, S_{-i} and a_j is 10, 10 and 3 respectively, a_j prefers to join S_{-i} since $D = 3$ when a_j joins S_{-i} whereas $D = 7$ if a_j does not join S_{-i}. Again, when the power of S_i, S_{-i} and a_j is 11, 8 and 4 respectively, a_j allies with S_{-i} since $D = 1$ when $a_j \epsilon S_{-i}$ while $D = 3$ if a_j does not ally with S_{-i}. On the other hand, if the power of S_i, S_{-i} and a_j is 7, 7 and 6 respectively, a_j does not ally with S_{-i} since $D = 6$ if a_j allies with S_{-i} whereas $D = 0$ if a_j does not ally with S_{-i}. If the power of S_i, S_{-i} and a_j is 12, 10 and 6 respectively, a_j again prefers to remain neutral rather than ally with S_{-i} since $D = 2$ if a_j remains neutral whereas $D = 4$ if a_j joins S_{-i}.

Summing up case 1, when all actors in the balancer version pursue equality policies, the theory is applicable only when $k_j \geqslant 2D$ or $k_j = D$.

The analyses of cases 2-8 (appendix B) are very similar to the analysis above. Table 4, however, summarizes the results of the balancer version's consistency and applicability when the two opposing alliances have unequal amounts of power. The types of foreign policy objectives and the power relations of a_j, S_i and S_{-i} are given in the left and right columns, respectively, of Table 4. In this table, the balancer version is consistent for each combination of policy objectives of the system's actors. The balancer version's two fixed axioms and every combination of axioms describing the policy objectives of S_i, S_{-i} and a_j are simultaneously satisfied when the power relations among S_i, and S_{-i} and a_j listed in Table 4 are met.

Table 4 also indicates that the applicability of this version varies for different combinations of policy objectives of the system's three actors. The results show that theoretical applicability depends to a large extent on the policy objectives that a_j, S_i and S_{-i} pursue. In all cases where the balancer nation adopts an equality policy (cases 1, 2, 3 and 5) the theory is applicable if $D = k_j$. Furthermore, when the more powerful alliance pursues an equality policy (cases 1, 3 and 4), the theory is also applicable if $k_j \geq 2D$. Note, however, when $k_j \geq 2D$ (cases 1, 3 and 4) the theory is applicable because the balancer nation *does not* ally with the weaker alliance. On the other hand, when the more powerful alliance pursues a hegemonic policy and $k_j \geq 2D$ (cases 2 and 5), axiom (2) is not satisfied since the balancer nation—in pursuing its equality policy objective—does not ally with the weaker side. Hence, the stress that traditional scholars have placed on a balancer nation pursuing an equality policy needs to be qualified. The findings here show that a balancer nation pursuing an equality policy objective does not always act as claimed in joining the weaker side (Herz, 1959; Lerche, 1956; Hassell, 1914; Churchill, 1948).

When the balancer nation and the more powerful alliance pursue hegemonic policies, the conditions for theoretical applicability are most restrictive (cases 7 and 8). The only set of *necessary and sufficient* conditions for theoretical applicability are: $D = k_j$ *and* $k_j > k(S_i)$. If $k_j > D$, axioms (1) and/or (2) are not satisfied and the theory is not applicable. If, on the other hand, the balancer nation pursues a hegemonic policy while the stronger alliance pursues an equality policy (cases 4 and 6), the theory is applicable under a larger number of conditions than when both the balancer nation and the stronger alliance pursue hegemonic policies.

It is interesting to interpret a couple of the situations examined above in the context of the "real world." One situation involves a balancer nation with hegemonic ambitions that chooses to remain neutral (see appendix B. subcases 7b.v and 8b.v). At first glance, such a decision appears counterintuitive. After all, a nation with hegemonic ambitions can only further its

TABLE 4

APPLICABILITY OF THE BALANCER VERSION
WHEN $k(S_i) > k(S_{-i})$

Case 1

S_i, S_{-i} and a_j pursue equality policies

Applicable when $k_j = D$ or $k_j \geq 2D$. Axiom (1) is not satisfied when $k_j < 2D$.

Case 2

S_{-i} and a_j pursue equality policies, S_i pursues a hegemonic policy

Applicable when $D = k_j$. Axiom (1) is not satisfied when $k_j < 2D$. Axiom (2) is not satisfied when $k_j \geq 2D$.

Case 3

S_i and a_j pursue equality policies, S_{-i} pursues a hegemonic policy

Applicable when $D = k_j$ or $k_j \geq 2D$. Axiom (1) is not satisfied when $k_j < 2D$.

Case 4

S_i and S_{-i} pursue equality policies, a_j pursues a hegemonic policy

Applicable when $D = k_j$ or $k_j \geq 2D$, or ($k_j < 2D$ and $k_j > k(S_i)$). Axiom (1) is not satisfied when $k_j < 2D$ and $k_j \leq k(S_i)$.

Case 5

S_i and S_{-i} pursue hegemonic policies, a_j pursues an equality policy.

Applicable when $D = k_j$. Axiom (1) is not satisfied when $k_j < 2D$. Axiom (2) is not satisfied when $k_j \geq 2D$.

Case 6

S_{-i} and a_j pursue hegemonic policies S_i pursues an equality policy.

Applicable when $D = k_j$. Axiom (1) is not satisfied when $k_j > D$ except when $k_j > k(S_i)$.

Case 7

S_i and a_j pursue hegemonic policies S_{-i} pursues an equality policy.

Applicable when $D = k_j$ and $k_j > k(S_{-i})$. Theory may be applicable when $k_j = D$ and $k_j < k(S_{-i})$. Axiom (1) is not satisfied when $k_j > D$ and sometimes axiom (2) is not satisfied.

Case 8

S_i, S_{-i} and a_j pursue hegemonic policies.

Applicable when $D = k_j$ and $k_j > k(S_{-i})$. Theory may be applicable when $k_j = D$ and $k_j < k(S_{-i})$. When $k_j > D$, axiom (1) is not satisfied and sometimes axiom (2) is not satisfied.

foreign policy objective by allying with other actors in the system. What kind of "real world" context or rationale can we provide for this nation's behavior? Quite simply, neutrality may be one means of "taking advantage of the quarrels of others to aggrandize oneself" (Wright, 1942:757). In fact, several writers have pointed out that the United States, by remaining neutral, was able to profit by the 1914-1917 war in Europe (Rippy, 1938: 21; Jessup, 1935:28).

It is also interesting to provide a "real world" context for the situation described by case 2. Here both the balancer nation and the weaker alliance pursue equality policies while the stronger alliance pursues a hegemonic policy. As a consequence of adopting an equality policy, the balancer remains neutral when $k_j \geqslant 2D$, but allies with the weaker alliance when $k_j < 2D$. What rationale can we provide for the balancer's behavior in this case? If one alliance is more powerful than its opponent and the more powerful alliance has hegemonic ambitions, war may break out between the two opponents. If war does break out, D may increase significantly if, for example, the weaker alliance grows weaker at a faster rate than the more powerful alliance. The net effect may be that the power of the balancer nation is $< 2D$. When the latter inequality holds, our model implies that the balancer nation allies with the weaker alliance. In fact, Wright (1942:784) notes that "great powers have usually been ready to enter wars when it appeared that the balance might be permanently disturbed by the victory of one side."

Table 4, then, shows that the balancer version of the theory is logically consistent when the two opposing alliances have unequal amounts of power. Its applicability is, however, more limited than when $k(S_i) = k(S_{-i})$. The belief that "it is highly desirable if not indispensable, that some state should be in a position to play the role of holder of the balance" (Kulski, 1964:12) in preventing the emergence of dominant actors, is correct only under the most restrictive sets of conditions. Axioms (1) and/or (2) are not satisfied for many of the conceivable power relations between S_i, S_{-i} and a_j.

SUMMARY

This chapter examined the consistency and applicability of the balancer version of the theory which consisted of fixed axioms (1) and (2), two opposing alliances that adopted either equality or hegemonic policies, and one neutral nation (the balancer nation) that adopted an equality or hegemonic policy. Although most writers have not placed restrictions on the initial power distribution among nations in the system, this analysis assumed that the initial power distribution was unequal. Thus, this research placed no restrictions on the power distribution between the two opposing alliances that formed. Consequently, the analysis consisted of two parts—the balancer version's consistency and applicability when the power of the two opposing alliances was equal, and this version's applicability when the power of the opposing alliances was unequal.

To demonstrate consistency it was necessary to show that a set of conditions existed under which the axioms of the theory were simultaneously satisfied. Many writers have argued that the existence of a balancer nation enhances the applicability of the balance of power theory. This analysis demonstrated that the applicability of the theory was fairly extensive when the power of the opposing alliances was equal. On the other hand, when unequal amounts of power were held by the two opposing alliances, the applicability of the theory proved to be fairly restrictive.

Not all writers, however, subscribe to the balancer version of the theory. As noted in chapter 2, two other versions of the theory are found in the traditional literature. Chapter 4 examines the consistency and applicability of these two additional variations of the balance of power theory.

4

CONSISTENCY AND APPLICABILITY OF THE EQUALITY AND HEGEMONIC VERSIONS

This chapter examines the consistency and applicability of the equality and hegemonic versions of the theory. As in the balancer version, these analyses assume that the initial distribution of power in the system is unequal. There is, then, at least one pair of nations, a_i and a_{-i}, such that $k_i > k_{-i}$. The dyad, a_i, a_{-i}, are the system's opposing nations.

However, these analyses differ from the balancer version in an important respect. The analysis of the balancer version began with a system in which all nations except one aligned with either a_i or a_{-i} to form two opposing alliances. Consequently, there were only three actors in the balancer version: two opposing alliances and one neutral nation. The focus in the balancer version was on the neutral nation's (i.e., the balancer nation's) decision to join an alliance.

The analyses of equality and hegemonic versions, on the other hand, begin with a system containing two opposing nations, a_i and a_{-i}, and n-2 nonaligned (or neutral) nations. There are, then, n-actors in the equality and hegemonic versions: two opposing nations and the system's remaining n-2 nations. The analyses of the equality and hegemonic versions examine the alliance patterns of the system's n-2 neutral nations.

In the equality version, the consistency and applicability of the theory are first examined when n-2 nations act in accordance with axiom (4) and a_i and a_{-i} act in accordance with axiom (3). To determine the consistency of this version, we must show the existence of *some* set of conditions under which fixed axioms (1) and (2), two opposing nations acting in accordance with axiom (3) and n-2 nations acting in accordance with axiom (4), are simultaneously satisfied. To determine the applicability of this version, we must specify the *entire* set of conditions under which axioms (1), (2), (3) and (4) are simultaneously satisfied.

The equality policy objectives of opposing and neutral nations (which are represented by axioms [3] and [4], respectively) require knowledge of the relationship between the power of the neutral nations,

$$A_j = (a_j : j=1, \ldots n-2),$$

and the difference in power between the system's opposing nations. The summed power of the neutral nations,

$$\sum_{j=1}^{n-2} k_j,$$

may be greater than, equal to, or less than the difference in power between the system's opposing nations, i.e.,

$$\sum_{j=1}^{n-2} k_j \underset{<}{\overset{>}{-}} d.$$

Each of these possibilities,

$$\sum_{j=1}^{n-2} k_j > d, \quad \sum_{j=1}^{n-2} k_j = d \text{ and } \sum_{j=1}^{n-2} k_j < d,$$

and their implications for the relationships between k_j, $j=1, \ldots n-2$, and d must therefore be examined.

The applicability of the equality version is first examined when *all* nations in the system pursue equality policies. That is, applicability is determined when a_i and a_{-i} pursue equality policies and the remaining n-2 nations pursue equality policies. The applicability of this version is then examined when some nations ($< n/2$) pursue hegemonic policies.

To examine the consistency and applicability of the hegemonic version, we first determine the conditions under which fixed axioms (1) and (2), two opposing nations acting in accordance with axiom (3'), and n-2 nations acting in accordance with axiom (4'), are simultaneously satisfied. We then examine the applicability of this version when some nations ($< n/2$) in the system pursue hegemonic policies.

Axioms (3') and (4'), which describe the hegemonic policies of opposing and neutral nations, require knowledge of the relationship between the power of the neutral nations and the difference in power between the system's opposing nations. The summed power of the neutral nations may be greater than, equal to, or less than the difference in power between the two opposing nations. These possibilities must therefore be considered here.

Axioms (3') and (4') also require knowledge of the relative power positions of the members of A_j and the system's opposing nations. k_j, $j=i$, $\ldots n-2$, may be greater than, equal to, or less than k_i and k_{-i}. In addition to considering the relationship between

$$\sum_{j=1}^{n-2} k_j \text{ and } d,$$

it is also necessary to examine the cases generated by the possible power relationships between a_j, $j=1 \ldots, n-2$, and a_i, a_{-i}.

This chapter is divided into four sections. Section I examines the consistency and applicability of the equality version when all nations in the system pursue equality policies. Section II studies the applicability of the equality version when a majority of nations pursue equality policies. Sections III and IV examine, respectively, the applicability and consistency of the hegemonic version when all nations pursue hegemonic policies and when a majority of nations in the system pursue hegemonic policies.

SECTION I
EQUALITY VERSION: ALL NATIONS
PURSUE EQUALITY POLICIES

Assumption 1
The initial power distribution in the system is assumed to be unequal so that there is at least one pair of nations, a_i and a_{-i}, such that $k_i > k_{-i}$. By definition, $k_i - k_{-i} = d > 0$. The dyad, a_i and a_{-i}, are the system's opposing nations.

Assumption 2
It is further assumed that a_i and a_{-i} act in accordance with axiom (3) and a_j ($j=1 \ldots .n-2$) act in accordance with axiom (4).

Assumption 3
Finally, it is assumed that

$$k_\varrho \ngtr \sum_{\ell \neq k}^{n} k(S_k)$$

so that the system does not initially contain a dominant actor.

The theory is consistent if conditions exist for which axioms (1), (2), (3) and (4) are simultaneously satisfied. The theory's applicability is known when all such conditions are specified.

To analyze the consistency and applicability of the equality version, it is necessary to consider the possible power relationships among the system's actors. The equality policies of the opposing and neutral nations (represented by axioms [3] and [4]) require knowledge of the relationship between the power of the n-2 neutral nations and the difference in power between the system's opposing nations. To make this analysis consistent with the presentation of the balancer version, the following possibilities are considered:

51

$$a.\ \sum_{\substack{j=1\\i\neq j}}^{n-2} k_j < d \qquad b.\ \sum_{\substack{j=1\\i\neq j}}^{n-2} k_j = d \qquad \text{and} \qquad c.\ \sum_{\substack{j=1\\i\neq j}}^{n-2} k_j > d.$$

The analysis below examines each of these possibilities and their implications for the relationships between k_j, (j=1, . . . n-2) and d.

Assume:

$$a.\ \sum_{\substack{j=1\\i\neq j}}^{n-2} k_j < d. \qquad d > \sum_{j=1}^{n-2} k_j \text{ implies that } k_i > k_{-i} + \Sigma k_j.$$

This inequality clearly contradicts assumption (3) which says that the system does not initially contain a dominant actor. This possibility is therefore excluded from further consideration.

Assume:

$$b.\ \sum_{\substack{j=1\\i\neq j}}^{n-2} k_j = d.$$

$d = \Sigma k_j$ implies that $\forall a_j \epsilon A_j$, $d > k_j$. In this case, a_j, j=1, . . n-2, ally with a_{-i} in accordance with axiom (4) since u_j, j=1, . . . n-2, increases when $|d|$ decreases. According to axiom (3), a_{-i} accepts a_j, j=1, ... n-2, as allies. Axioms (1), (2), (3) and (4) are simultaneously satisfied.

Assume:

$$c.\ \sum_{\substack{j=1\\i\neq j}}^{n-2} k_j > d.$$

$\Sigma k_j > d$ implies that $\forall a_j$ ($k_j < d$ or $k_j = d$ or $k_j > d$). Axioms (3) and (4) require an examination of each of these possibilities.

Before continuing the analysis, a review of Figure 1 is helpful. When a member of A_j allies with a_{-i}, alliance S_{-i} is formed. Likewise, if a member of A_j allies with a_i, alliance S_i is formed. The difference in power between the two opposing actors is computed at each stage of the alliance formation process. For example, if a_j allies with a_{-i}, the difference in power between the two opposing actors is now calculated by $k_i - (k_{-i} + k_j)$. Furthermore, $k_{-i} + k_j = k(S_{-i})$ and $k_i - k(S_{-i}) = D$. As soon as a nation allies with one of the opposing nations, the difference in power between the opposing actors is recalculated and is represented by D.

We now consider each of the possible relationships implied by (c).

c.1. $k_j < d$ (or $k_j < D$ after some members of A_j have allied with a_i or a_{-i} to form two opposing alliances)

At any stage in the process of alliance formation, any $a_j \epsilon A_j$ satisfying $k_j < d$ (or $k_j < D$) ally with a_{-j} (or S_{-j}) to decrease the difference in power between the two opposing actors.

c.2. $k_j = d$ (or $k_j = D$)

If there exists ($\exists$) an a_j at any stage in the alliance formation process such that $k_j = d$ or $k_j = D$, the process of alliance formation terminates and the theory is applicable. Furthermore, $k(S_i) = k(S_{-i})$.

c.3. $k_j > d$ (or $k_j > D$)

If $k_j > d$ (or $k_j > D$) at any stage in the process of alliance formation, then any $a_j \epsilon A_j$ satisfying

c.3.1. $k_j < 2d$ (or $k_j < 2D$)

ally with the weaker opponent. When (*c.3.1*) is satisfied, the difference in power between the two opponents is less than what it was prior to the increased membership(s). [For a more thorough discussion of this case, see case *1.c* of the balancer version when $k(S_i) > k(S_{-i})$.]

On the other hand, any $a_j \epsilon A_j$ satisfying

c.3.2. $k_j \geqslant 2d$ (or $k_j \geqslant 2D$)

do not ally with the weaker opponent, but remain neutral. In allying with the weaker opponent, they would thereby increase the difference in power between the two opponents—a result which is not compatible with the policy objectives they pursue. [For a more detailed discussion of this, see case *1.c* of the balancer version when $k(S_i) > k(S_{-i})$.]

Cases (*a*), (*b*), (*c.1*), (*c.2*), (*c.3.1*) and (*c.3.2*) describe the relationships that may exist between the power of the neutral nations and the system's opposing actors for any stage of the alliance formation process. Case (*a*) is excluded by assumption (3) of this analysis. If the relationship expressed by (*b*) is satisfied, all a_j, j=1, . . . n-2 ally with a_{-i} and $k_i = k(S_{-i}) \vee a_j \epsilon S_{-i}$ and the theory is applicable. All $a_j \epsilon A_j$ that satisfy (*c.1*) or (*c.3.1*) ally with a_{-i} (or S_{-i}) to decrease the difference in power between the opposing actors. If there is an $a_j \epsilon A_j$ that satisfies (*c.2*), a_j allies with a_{-i} (or S_{-i}) and the process of alliance formation terminates. Finally, all $a_j \epsilon A_j$ that satisfy (*c.3.2*) choose to remain neutral rather than ally with one of the opposing actors.

Briefly then, if conditions (*b*) or (*c.2*) are satisfied, the process of alliance formation ends and the power of opposing actors is equal. On the other hand, those members of A_j that satisfy (*c.1*) or (*c.3.1*) proceed to ally with the weaker opponent. Lastly, those members of A_j who satisfy (*c.3.2*) do not join S_i or S_{-i} but remain neutral.

The theory is applicable if condition (*b*) or (*c.2*) is satisfied. In both cases, axioms (1), (2), (3) and (4) are simultaneously satisfied and the power of the opposing actors is equal. The theory is also applicable if condition (*c.3.2*) is satisfied. All $a_j \epsilon A_j$ satisfying condition (*c.3.2*) do not ally with either opponent. Although one alliance is stronger than its opponent, axiom (2) is satisfied because the more powerful alliance pursues an equality policy. The only condition for which this version of the theory is inapplicable is when all nations except one are allied with one of the opposing actors and the single nonaligned nation satisfies condition $(c.1)$ or $(c.3.1)$. In other words, the theory is inapplicable when all nations except one (the balancer nation) are members of an alliance, and the power of the balancer is less than D (i.e., $k_j < D$). When $k_j < D$, the balancer nation allies with the weaker opponent. Axiom (1) is violated since S_{-i} is now a dominant actor in the system.

In sum, when all nations in the system pursue equality policies, the theory is applicable under all conditions except when all but one nation (the balancer nation) are members of an alliance and the power of the balancer nation is less than D.

This version of the theory is clearly consistent since any combination of power relationships between neutral nations and opposing actors (except the relationship described above) simultaneously satisfy axioms (1), (2), (3) and (4).

SECTION II
APPLICABILITY OF EQUALITY VERSION WHEN THE MAJORITY OF NATIONS PURSUE EQUALITY POLICIES

In contrast to a system where all nations pursue equality policies, suppose we have a system where some nations ($< n/2$) pursue hegemonic policies. It is now possible for a_i (or S_i), a_{-i} (or S_{-i}) and members of A_j to pursue hegemonic policies. How does this affect the applicability of the theory? When we allow for these possibilities, the number of conditions under which the theory is inapplicable increases. The conditions for inapplicability are found in the balancer analysis in Table 4 which examines the behavior of a single neutral nation who pursues an equality or hegemonic policy in a system where the opposing alliances pursue equality or hegemonic policies. This section examines the behavior of n-2 neutral nations who pursue either equality or hegemonic policies in a system where the opposing actors pursue equality or hegemonic policies. The major modification of the results in Table 4 is that they include all $a_j \epsilon A_j$ instead of a single member of A_j. The conditions for *inapplicability* are:

1. All but one nation (the balancer nation) are members of an alliance, the balancer nation pursues an equality policy and the power of the balancer nation is less than D.

54

This condition is the same as the condition found in section I for theoretical inapplicability. If condition (1) occurs in a system where all nations pursue equality policies, it surely may occur in a system where the majority of nations pursue equality policies.

2. S_i pursues a hegemonic policy, $k(S_i) > k(S_{-i})$.
$\forall a_j$ pursuing equality policies, $k_j \geq 2D$ and $- \exists a_j$ pursuing a hegemonic policy such that $k_j = D$.

Axiom (2) is not satisfied if this condition holds. (See case 5 of the balancer version for a_j pursuing an equality policy and case 7 for a_j pursuing a hegemonic policy in Table 4.)

3. S_i pursues a hegemonic policy, $k(S_i) > k(S_{-i})$, and $\exists a_j$ pursuing a hegemonic policy such that $D > k_j$.

$D > k_j$ implies that $k_j \leq k(S_{-i})$ or $k_j > k(S_{-i})$. If $k_j \leq k(S_{-i})$, a_j allies with S_i in accordance with axiom (4'). On the other hand, if $k_j > k(S_{-i})$, a_j remains neutral (again, in accordance with axiom [4']). In both cases, axiom (2) is not satisfied.

4. S_i pursues a hegemonic policy, $k(S_i) > k(S_{-i})$, and $\exists a_j$ pursuing a hegemonic policy such that: $k_j > D$ and $[(k_j < k(S_i)$ and $k_j < k(S_{-i})$ and $k_j \geq 2D)$ or $(k_j < k(S_i)$ and $k_j = k(S_{-i})$ and $k_j \geq 2D)$ or $(k_j > k(S_i) > k(S_{-i}))]$.

(See the analysis of case 7b in appendix B.) If there is an a_j that pursues a hegemonic policy and satisfies any of these conditions, a_j allies with S_i and axiom (2) is not satisfied.

The number of conditions under which this version is inapplicable increases as nations are permitted to pursue hegemonic policies. When all nations in the system pursue equality policies (section I), condition (1) is the only condition for which the theory is inapplicable. As soon as some nations in the system are allowed to pursue hegemonic policies, the number of conditions under which the theory is inapplicable increases from one to four.

SECTION III
HEGEMONIC VERSION: ALL NATIONS
PURSUE HEGEMONIC POLICIES

Assumption 1
The initial power distribution in the system is assumed to be unequal so that there is at least one pair of nations, a_i and a_{-i}, such that, $k_i > k_{-i}$. By definition, $k_i - k_{-i} = d > 0$. The dyad, a_i and a_{-i}, are the system's opposing nations.

Assumption 2

It is further assumed that a_i and a_{-i} act in accordance with axiom $(3')$ and a_j $(j=1,\ldots n-2)$ act in accordance with axiom $(4')$.

Assumption 3

Finally, it is assumed that

$$k_i \not> \sum_{\substack{i\neq k}}^{n} k(S_k)$$

so that the system does not initially contain a dominant actor.

The theory is consistent if conditions exist for which axioms (1), (2), $(3')$ and $(4')$ are simultaneously satisfied. The theory's applicability is known when all such conditions are specified.

The hegemonic policy of opposing nations (axiom $[3']$) requires knowledge of the relationship between the power of the n-2 neutral nations and the difference in power between the system's opposing nations. To make this analysis consistent with the presentation of the equality version in section I, the following possibilities are considered:

$$a.\ \sum_{\substack{j=1\\i\neq j}}^{n-2} k_j < d \qquad b.\ \sum_{\substack{j=1\\i\neq j}}^{n-2} k_j = d \qquad \text{and} \qquad c.\ \sum_{\substack{j=1\\i\neq j}}^{n-2} k_j > d.$$

Axiom $(4')$, which describes the hegemonic policy of neutral nations, requires knowledge of the relative power positions of the members of A_j and the system's opposing nations. $k_j, j=1,\ldots n-2,$ may be greater than, equal to or less than k_i and k_{-i}. That is, $\forall a_j \epsilon A_j$,

$$(k_j \overset{>}{_<} k_i \text{ and/or } k_j \overset{>}{_<} k_{-i}).$$

The analysis below considers each of the following possibilities,

$$a.\ \sum_{\substack{j=1\\i\neq j}}^{n-2} k_j < d, \qquad b.\ \sum_{\substack{j=1\\i\neq j}}^{n-2} k_j = d, \qquad \text{and} \qquad c.\ \sum_{\substack{j=1\\i\neq j}}^{n-2} k_j > d,$$

and their implications for the relationships between $k_j, j=1,\ldots n-2, k_i$ and k_{-i}.

Briefly, the cases considered below are generated as follows: possibilities (a), (b) and (c) each imply a set of relationships between k_j and d for all members of A_j. (Axiom $[3']$ requires us to consider the relationships between k_j and d for all members of A_j.) These relationships are presented in (a), (b1), (c1), (c2), and (c3). Cases (b1), (c1), (c2) and (c3) imply, in turn, a set of relationships among k_j, $j=1, \ldots n-2$, k_i and k_{-i}. (Axiom [4'] requires us to consider the relationships among k_j, $j=1, \ldots n-2$, k_i and k_{-i}.) As a result of these considerations, the analysis below examines 13 cases— (a), (b1.i), (b1.ii), (c1.i), (c1.ii), (c2.i), (c2.ii), (c2.iii), (c3.i), (c3.ii), (c3.iii), (c3.iv), (c3.v).

Assume:

$$a. \quad \sum_{\substack{j=1 \\ i \neq j}}^{n-2} k_j < d \qquad d > \sum_{j=1}^{n-2} k_j \text{ implies that } k_i > k_{-i} + \Sigma k_j.$$

This inequality clearly contradicts assumption (3) which says that the system does not initially contain a dominant actor. This possibility is therefore excluded from further consideration.

Assume:

$$b. \quad \sum_{j=1}^{n-2} k_j = d. \qquad d = \Sigma k_j \text{ implies that (b1) } \forall a_j \epsilon A_j, d > k_j.$$

To determine the behavior of $a_j \epsilon A_j$, axiom (4') requires additional information regarding the power relationships between the members of A_j, and a_i, a_{-i}. Case (b1) implies that $\forall a_j \epsilon A_j, [k_j < k_i \text{ and } (k_j \leqslant k_{-i} \text{ or } k_j > k_{-i})]$. Axiom (4') requires an examination of each of these possibilities.

Before resuming the analysis, it is helpful to review some of the notations in Figure 1. When a member of A_j allies with a_{-i}, alliance S_{-i} is formed. Likewise, if a member of A_j allies with a_i, alliance S_i is formed. The difference in power between the two opposing actors is computed at each stage of the alliance formation process. For example, if a_j allies with a_{-i}, the difference in power between the two opposing actors is now calculated by $k_i - (k_{-i} + k_j)$. Furthermore, $k_{-i} + k_j = k(S_{-i})$ and $k_i - k(S_{-i}) = D$. As soon as a nation allies with one of the opposing nations, the difference in power between the opposing actors is recalculated and represented by D.

We now consider each of the possible relationships implied by (b1).

(b1.i) $k_j \leqslant k_{-i}$ [or $k_j \leqslant k(S_{-i})$] after some members of A_j have allied with a_i or a_{-i} to form two opposing alliances)

Recall that (b) implies $\forall a_j \epsilon A_j, [d(D) > k_j \text{ and } k_i > k_j \text{ (or } k(S_i) > k_j)]$. According to axiom (4'), all $a_j \epsilon A_j$ satisfying (b1.i) ally with a_i (S_i). These members of A_j become more powerful than a_{-i} (or S_{-i}) since they substitute the power of the newly formed alliance for their own in calculating their relative power positions. According to axiom (3'), a_i (or S_i) accepts these members of A_j as allies. If any $a_j \epsilon A_j$ satisfy (b1.i) at any stage in the alliance formation process, axiom (2) is not satisfied.

(b1.ii) $k_j > k_{-i}$ [or $k_j > k (S_{-i})$]

According to axiom (4'), members of A_j that satisfy (b1.ii) prefer to remain neutral. They cannot improve their relative power positions with respect to the system's opposing actors by joining an alliance. If $\exists a_j \epsilon A_j$ that satisfies (b1.ii), axiom (2) is not satisfied [since a_i (or S_i) pursues a hegemonic policy and is stronger than a_{-i} (S_{-i})].

Assume:

$$c. \quad \sum_{\substack{j=1 \\ j \neq i}}^{n-2} k_j > d \qquad \Sigma k_j > d \text{ implies that } \forall a_j \epsilon A_j \ [k_j < d \ (D) \text{ or}$$

$k_j = d$ (D) or $k_j > d$ (D)]. Axiom (3') requires an examination of each of these possibilities.

(c1) $k_j < d$ (D)

Axiom (4') requires additional information regarding the power relationships between the members of A_j and a_i (S_i) and a_{-i} (S_{-i}). $k_j < d$ (D) implies that $\forall a_j \epsilon A_j, \{k_j < k_i \ [k \ (S_i)] \text{ and } k_j \leqslant k_{-i} \ [k \ (S_{-i})] \text{ or } k_j > k_{-i} \ [k \ (S_{-i})]\}$. each of these possibilities must also be considered.

(c1.i) $k_j < d$ (D) and $k_j \leqslant k_{-i}$ [or k (S_{-i})]

This condition is identical to condition (b1.i). The analysis is therefore the same as in (b1.i). Any members of A_j satisfying (c1.i) ally with $a_i(S_i)$ and axiom (2) is not satisfied.

(c1.ii) $k_j < d$ (D) and $k_j > k_{-i}$ [or k (S_{-i})]

This condition is identical to condition (b1.ii) above. As in (b1.ii), if $\exists a_j \epsilon A_j$ that satisfies (c1.ii), axiom (2) is not satisfied.

(c2) $k_j = d$ (or $k_j = D$)

Axiom (4') requires knowledge of the relative power positions of the members of A_j and the system's opposing actors. $k_j = d$ (or D) implies that

$$\forall a_j \epsilon A_j, k_i > k_j \ [\text{or } k \ (S_i) > k_j] \text{ and } [k_j \underset{<}{\overset{>}{-}} k_{-i}] \ [\text{or } k_j \underset{<}{\overset{>}{-}} k(S_{-i})].$$

Each of these possibilities is therefore examined below.

(c2.i) $k_j = d$ (D) and $k_j > k_{-i}$ [or $k_j > k (S_{-i})$] and $k_i > k_j$ [or k $(S_i) > k_j$].

According to axiom (4'), all members of A_j that satisfy (c2.i) at any stage in the alliance formation process ally with a_{-i} (or S_{-i}). By allying with a_{-i} (S_{-i}), they improve their relative power position with respect to a_i (S_i). By axiom (3'), a_{-i} (S_{-i}) accepts these nations as allies. As a result, the power of opposing actors is equal since $k_j = d$ (D).

(c2.ii) $k_j = d$ (D) and $k_i > k_j$ [or $k(S_i) > k_j$] and $k_j = k_{-i}$ [or $k_j = k(S_{-i})$].

Members of A_j that satisfy (c2.ii) improve their relative power positions by allying with either a_i (S_i) or a_{-i} (S_{-i}) (by axiom [4']). If they ally with a_i (S_i), they improve their relative power positions with respect to a_{-i} (S_{-i}). On the other hand, if they ally with a_{-i} (S_{-i}), they improve their relative power positions with respect to a_i (S_i). If *any* member of A_j that satisfies (c2.ii) allies with a_i (S_i) axiom (2) is not satisfied. However, if all members of A_j satisfying (c2.ii) ally with a_i (S_{-i}), the theory may be applicable.

(c2.iii) $k_j = d$ (D) and $k_i > k_j$ [or $k(S_i) > k_j$] and $k_j < k_{-i}$ [or $k_j < k(S_{-i})$].

Members of A_j that satisfy (c2.iii) improve their relative power positions by allying with either a_i (S_i) or a_{-i} (S_{-i}) according to axiom (4'). If they ally with a_i (S_i), they improve their relative power positions with respect to a_{-i} (S_{-i}). However, if they ally with a_{-i} (S_{-i}), they improve their relative power positions with respect to a_i (S_i). If *any* member of A_j that satisfies (c2.iii) allies with a_i (S_i), axiom (2) is not satisfied. On the other hand, if all members of A_j satisfying (c2.iii) ally with a_{-i} (S_{-i}), the theory may be applicable.

(c3) $k_j > d$ (D).

Axiom (4') requires additional information concerning the power relationships between the members of A_j and a_i (S_i) and a_{-i}(S_{-i}). $k_j > d$ (D) implies that

$$\forall a_j \epsilon A_j \; [k_j \overset{>}{\underset{<}{-}} k_i \text{ or } k_j \overset{>}{\underset{<}{-}} k(S_i) \text{ and } k_j \overset{>}{\underset{<}{-}} k_{-i} \text{ or } k_j \overset{>}{\underset{<}{-}} k(S_{-i})].$$

Each of these possibilities is therefore examined below.

(c3.i) $k_j > d$ (D) and $k_j < k_i$ [or $k_j < k(S_i)$] and $k_j > k_{-i}$ [or $k_j > k(S_{-i})$].

According to axiom (4'), members of A_j that satisfy (c3.i) ally with a_{-i} (S_{-i}) to improve their relative power positions with respect to a_i (S_i). In accordance with axiom (3'), a_{-i} (S_{-i}) accept these members of A_j as allies. If condition (c3.i) is satisfied by all members of A_j, axiom (1) is not satisfied since S_{-i} becomes a dominant actor.

(c3.ii) $k_j > d$ (D) and $k_j = k_i$ [or $k_j = k(S_i)$] and $k_j > k_{-i}$ [or $k_j > k(S_{-i})$].

According to axiom (4'), members of A_j that satisfy (c3.ii) ally with a_{-i} (S_{-i}) to improve their relative power positions with respect to a_i (S_i). In accordance with axiom (3'), a_{-i} (S_{-i}) accept these members of A_j as allies.

If condition (c3.ii) is satisfied by all members of A_j, axiom (1) is not satisfied since S_{-i} becomes a dominant actor.

(c3.iii) $k_j > d$ (D) and $k_j < k_i$ [or $k_j < k(S_i)$] and $k_j < k_{-i}$ [or $k_j < k(S_{-i})$].

Members of A_j satisfying (c3.iii) ally with either a_i (S_i) or a_{-i} (S_{-i}) (by axiom [4']). If they ally with a_i (S_i), they improve their relative power positions with respect to a_{-i} (S_{-i}). On the other hand, if they ally with a_{-i} (S_{-i}), they improve their relative power positions with respect to a_i (S_i). According to axiom (3'), both a_i (S_i) and a_{-i} (S_{-i}) are willing to accept these members of A_j as allies. Axiom (2) is not satisfied if *any* member of A_j satisfying (c3.iii) allies with a_i (S_i). If all members of A_j satisfy (c3.iii), axiom (1) is violated.

(c3.iv) $k_j > d$ (D) and $k_j < k_i$ [or $k_j < k(S_i)$] and $k_j = k_{-i}$ [or $k_j = k(S_{-i})$].

Members of A_j satisfying (c3.iv) ally with either a_i (S_i) or a_{-i} (S_{-i}) by axiom [4']). If they ally with a_i (S_i), they improve their relative power positions with respect to a_{-i} (S_{-i}). On the other hand, if they ally with a_{-i} (S_{-i}), they improve their relative power positions with respect to a_i (S_i). According to axiom (3'), both a_i (S_i) and a_{-i} (S_{-i}) are willing to accept these members of A_j as allies. Axiom (2) is not satisfied if *any* member of A_j satisfying (c3.iv) allies with a_i (S_i). If all members of A_j satisfy (c3.iv), axiom (1) is violated.

(c3.v) $k_j > d$ (D) and $k_j > k_i > k_{-i}$ [or $k_j > k(S_i) > k(S_{-i})$].

According to axiom (4'), members of A_j that satisfy (c3.v) prefer to remain neutral. They cannot improve their relative power positions with respect to the system's opposing actors by joining in an alliance with either opponent. If $\exists a_j \epsilon A_j$ that satisfies (c3.v), axiom (2) is not satisfied because a_i (S_i) pursues a hegemonic policy and is stronger than a_{-i} (S_{-i}).

At this point, our analysis of the consistency and applicability of the hegemonic version has led us to examine twelve cases. The results are recorded in Table 5.

For the cases in quadrants I and II of Table 5, the hegemonic version is not consistent. Any member of A_j that satisfies (b1.i) or (c1.i) in quadrant I allies with the more powerful actor pursuing a hegemonic policy. As a result, axiom (2) is violated. On the other hand, any member of A_j that satisfies (b1.ii), (c1.ii) or (c3.v) in quadrant II remains neutral. By not allying with the weaker opponent, axiom (2) is again violated and consequently the theory is not consistent. It is therefore unnecessary to consider further the cases in quadrants I and II.

TABLE 5
CASES CONSIDERED IN HEGEMONIC VERSION

I. *Ally with a_i (S$_i$)*	II. *Remain Neutral*
Cases: (b1.i)	Cases: (b1.ii)
(c1.i)	(c1.ii)
	(c3.v)

III. *Ally with a_{-i} (S$_{-i}$)*	IV. *Ally with Either*
Cases: (c2.i)	*a_i (S$_i$) or a_{-i} (S$_{-i}$)*
(c3.i)	Cases: (c2.ii)
(c3.ii)	(c2.iii)
	(c3.iii)
	(c3.iv)

For the cases in quadrant IV, members of A_j ally with either a_i (S_i) or a_{-i} (S_{-i}). If any member of A_j allies with a_i (S_i), axiom (2) is violated. On the other hand, if all members of A_j that satisfy conditions in quadrant IV ally with a_{-i} (S_{-i}), axiom (2) is satisfied. However, both axioms (1) and (2) must be satisfied if the theory is consistent. We now need to consider whether axiom (1) is also satisfied in these cases.

The same consideration arises for the cases in quadrant III. Members of A_j satisfying conditions in quadrant III ally with the weaker opponent. In doing so, axiom (2) is satisfied. But the question remains as to whether axiom (1) is also satisfied when members of A_j ally with the weaker opponent. It is therefore necessary to find the conditions under which both axioms (1) and (2) are satisfied for the cases in quadrants III and IV.

To determine these conditions, the cases in quadrants III and IV are regrouped according to the relationship between k_j and d (D). In all subcases of (c3), $k_j > d$ (D) and in all subcases of (c2), $k_j = d$ (D). The subcases of (c3) comprise one group and the subcases of (c2) comprise a second group. Let us first discuss the subcases of (c3).

Members of A_j ally with the weaker opponent (S_{-i}) in case (c3.ii), quadrant III. Suppose that all members of A_j satisfying conditions in (c3.iii) and (c3.iv), quadrant IV, also ally with the weaker opponent. The result is that the power between opposing actors is unequal [because $k_j > d(D)$]. Let us also suppose that inequality persists through all stages of the alliance formation process. That is, every time a member of A_j allies with one of the opposing actors, that actor becomes more powerful than its opponent.

(Axiom [2] is violated if the opposing actor, already more powerful, increases its power vis-à-vis the opponent.) However, if each of the remaining members of A_j allies with the weaker opponent, thereby making it stronger, axiom (1) is not satisfied because the power of one of the two actors is always greater than the other. Consequently, if a situation of inequality persists through all stages of the alliance formation process, there are no conditions under which both axioms (1) and (2) are satisfied.

In all subcases of (c2), $k_j = d$ (D). Any member of A_j that satisfies conditions in (c2.i), quadrant IV, allies with the weaker opponent and the power of opposing actors is equal. Furthermore, when any member of A_j satisfies conditions in (c2.ii) or (c2.iii), quadrant IV, the power of opposing actors may become equal if that nation allies with the weaker opponent. Once a situation of equality is established between opposing actors, both axioms (1) and (2) are satisfied. There is obviously no dominant actor in the system because $k(S_i) = k(S_{-i})$, satisfying axiom (1). Furthermore, axiom (2) cannot be violated because we have established that the power of opposing actors is equal. The only means by which axioms (1) and (2) are violated is if the remaining members of A_j ally with one of the opposing actors, thereby changing the power relationship from equality to inequality. On the other hand, if equality is established and persists, axioms (1) and (2) are simultaneously satisfied. The question remains then: under what conditions does a situation of equality between opposing actors endure? We turn now to an analysis of these conditions.

Assumptions: Assume that some member of A_j allies with the weaker opponent so that $k(S_i) = k(S_{-i})$. [That is, some $a_j \epsilon A_j$ satisfies conditions in (c2.i) or conditions in (c2.ii) or (c2.iii) and allies with the weaker opponent]. Assume further that there are some members of A_j left in the system.

Question: Under what conditions do members of A_j remain neutral so that $k(S_i) = k(S_{-i})$ endures?

Analysis: Axiom (3') requires knowledge of the relationship between k_j and D for all members of A_j. In this case, D = 0, so that $\forall a_j \epsilon A_j$ $(k_j > D)$. Axiom (4') requires us to consider the relationship between k_j, $k(S_i)$ and $k(S_{-i})$. It is therefore necessary to consider the following possibilities: (1) $k_j > k(S_i)$, (2) $k_j = k(S_i)$ and (3) $k_j < k(S_i)$.

1. Assume $k_j > k(S_i)$.

According to axiom (4'), any member of A_j that satisfies (1) remains neutral because it cannot improve its relative power position with respect to the system's opposing alliances. If all remaining members of A_j satisfy (1), equality between opposing actors endures and both axioms (1) and (2) are satisfied.

2. Assume $k_j = k(S_i)$.

According to axiom (4'), any members of A_j that satisfy (2) ally with either S_i or S_{-i}. By allying with S_{-i}, they improve their relative power position with respect to S_i. On the other hand, if they ally with S_i, they improve their relative power position with respect to S_{-i}. According to axiom (3'), both alliances are willing to accept additional members. As a result, the relationship between opposing alliances changes from equality to inequality. If inequality endures, both axioms (1) and (2) are not satisfied.

3. Assume $k_j < k(S_i)$.

According to axiom (2), any members of A_j that satisfy (3) ally with either S_{-i} or S_i. By allying with S_{-i}, they improve their relative power position with respect to S_i. Similarly, if they ally with S_i, they improve their relative power position with respect to S_{-i}. According to axiom (3'), both alliances are willing to accept additional members. As a result, the relationship between opposing actors changes from equality to inequality. If inequality persists, both axioms (1) and (2) are not satisfied.

Case 1 above identifies the only conditions under which a situation of equality between opposing actors, once established, endures. Once a situation of equality is established, the power of *every* neutral nation must be greater than the power of the opposing actors.

Summarizing section III, we find that the hegemonic version of the theory is applicable under the following conditions:

1. $\exists a_j \epsilon A_j$ that satisfies (c2.i) $[k_j = d(D)$ and $k_j > k(S_{-i})]$ and $[k_j > k(S_i) = k(S_{-i})]$ for all remaining members of A_j.

The first part of condition (1) (i.e., $\exists a_j \epsilon A_j$), establishes equality of power between opposing actors. If the second part of this condition is satisfied, equality between opposing actors endures.

2. $\exists a_j \epsilon A_j$ that satisfies (c2.ii) or (c2.iii) $[k_j = D$ and $k_j \leqslant k(S_{-i})]$ and a_j allies with the weaker actor. Additionally, all remaining members of A_j satisfy $[k_j > k(S_i) = k(S_{-i})]$.

The first part of condition (2) establishes equality between opposing actors while the second part of this condition insures that equality, once established, endures. Note that in the first part of (2), a_j, in addition to satisfying (c2.ii) or (c2.iii), is also required to ally with the weaker opponent.

Conditions (1) and (2) are the only conditions for which this version is applicable. Note too that they are restrictive conditions. If there is no member of A_j whose power is equal to the difference in power between the opposing actors at some stage in the alliance formation process, the theory is inapplicable. Moreover, even if there is a member of A_j whose power is equal to the difference in power between opposing actors, the power of every remaining member of A_j must be greater than the power of the opposing actors.

However, the existence of conditions (1) and (2) permits us to conclude that the hegemonic version is consistent. To show consistency, it is only necessary to demonstrate that some condition exists for which all axioms of the theory are simultaneously satisfied. Axioms (1), (2), (two opposing nations acting in accordance with) axiom (3') and (n-2 nations acting in accordance with) axiom (4') are simultaneously satisfied under conditions (1) or (2). It is worth noting that these conclusions conflict with those reached earlier by Riker (1962:159-87).

SECTION IV
APPLICABILITY OF HEGEMONIC VERSION WHEN THE MAJORITY OF NATIONS PURSUE HEGEMONIC POLICIES

In contrast to a system where all nations pursue hegemonic policies, suppose we have a system where some nations $(< n/2)$ pursue equality policies. It is now possible for a_i (or S_i), a_{-i} (or S_{-i}) and members of A_j to pursue equality policies. When we allow for these possibilities, the number of conditions under which the theory is applicable increases. The conditions for applicability are obtained for the most part by examining the results of the balancer analyses in Tables 3 and 4. The balancer analysis examines the behavior of a single neutral nation that pursues an equality or hegemonic policy in a system where the two opposing alliances pursue equality or hegemonic policies. This section examines the behavior of n-2 neutral nations that pursue equality or hegemonic policies in a system where the opposing actors pursue equality or hegemonic policies. The major modification of the results in Tables 3 and 4 is that they include all $a_j \epsilon A_j$ instead of a single member of A_j. The conditions for applicability are:

1. $\exists a_j \epsilon A_j$ with a hegemonic policy that satisfies $[k_j = D$ and $k_j > k(S_{-i})]$ and $[k_j > k(S_i) = k(S_{-i})]$ for all remaining members of A_j that pursue hegemonic policies.

This condition is similar to condition (1) of section III. The major difference is that the above condition is less restrictive than the condition of section III. Note that the second part of this condition $[k_j > k(S_i) = k(S_{-i})]$ applies only to those remaining members of A_j with hegemonic policies. Once equality between opposing actors is established, members of A_j with equality policies do not ally with either opponent (see Table 3, case 3).

2. $\exists a_j \epsilon A_j$ with a hegemonic policy that satisfies $[k_j = D$ and $k_j \leqslant k(S_{-i})]$ and a_j allies with a weaker opponent. Additionally,

all remaining members of A_j with hegemonic policies satisfy $[k_j > k(S_i) = k(S_{-i})]$.

This condition is similar to condition (2) of section III. As in condition (1), the major difference between this condition and condition (2) of section III is that the latter condition is more restrictive.

    3. S_i and S_{-i} pursue hegemonic policies.

        a. $\exists a_j \epsilon A_j$ that pursues an equality policy and satisfies $k_j = D$, or

        b. $\exists a_j \epsilon A_j$ with a hegemonic policy that satisfies $[k_j = D$ and $k_j > k(S_{-i})]$ and

        c. all remaining members of A_j pursue equality policies.

If this condition holds, an equal distribution of power between opposing actors is established and it endures. Power parity is established by (*a*) or (*b*) above. [Refer to (c2.i) in section III to see how equality is established between opposing actors by a neutral nation pursuing a hegemonic policy. To see how equality is established between opposing actors by a neutral nation pursuing an equality policy, refer to case 5 in Table 4.] Power parity persists because all remaining members of A_j pursue equality policies. (Refer to case 3, Table 3, to see why equality persists.)

    4. S_i pursues an equality policy, $k(S_i) > k(S_{-i})$,

        a. All remaining members of A_j that pursue equality policies satisfy, $k_j \geqslant 2D$ or $k_j = D$, and

        b. All remaining members of A_j that pursue hegemonic policies satisfy, $k_j > k(S_i) > k(S_{-i})$.

If (*a*) and (*b*) in condition (4) hold, all remaining neutral nations maintain their neutrality. (To see the behavior of neutral nations pursuing hegemonic policies, see case 6 in Table 4, and look at case 3, Table 4 to see the behavior of neutral nations pursuing equality policies.) It is therefore possible to satisfy axiom (1). Furthermore, because the more powerful opposing actor pursues an equality policy, neutral nations can maintain their neutrality without violating axiom (2).

The number of conditions under which this version is applicable increases as some nations are permitted to pursue equality policies. When all nations in the system pursue hegemonic policies, conditions (1) and (2) in section III are the only conditions for which the theory is applicable. As soon as some nations in the system are allowed to pursue equality policies, the number of conditions under which the theory is applicable increases from two to four.

SUMMARY

This chapter examined the consistency and applicability of the equality and hegemonic versions of the balance of power theory. The equality version assumed that all actors in the system, both nations and alliances, pursued equality policies. It consisted of the following set of axioms: fixed axioms (1) and (2), two opposing nations acting in accordance with axiom (3), and n-2 neutral nations acting in accordance with axiom (4). The hegemonic version, on the other hand, assumed that all actors (nations and alliances) pursued hegemonic policies. The hegemonic version consisted of fixed axioms (1) and (2), two opposing nations acting in accordance with axiom (3'), and n-2 nations acting in accordance with axiom (4').

Analyses were then done to find the conditions under which each set of axioms was simultaneously satisfied. To demonstrate consistency, it was only necessary to show that some set of conditions existed under which the axioms of the theory were simultaneously satisfied. To determine each version's applicability, it was necessary to identify the entire set of conditions under which the axioms of each version were simultaneously satisfied.

We found that the equality version was not only consistent but that its applicability was extensive. Only one condition was found under which the theory's axioms were not satisfied. We therefore concluded that all other power relationships between opposing and neutral actors satisfied the set of axioms. We then modified the equality version somewhat to see what effect this modification had on its applicability. Specifically, we allowed some nations in the system to pursue hegemonic policies. As a result, additional conditions were found which violated some of the theory's axioms. Therefore, the applicability of the equality version decreased when some nations in the system were allowed to pursue hegemonic policies.

The consistency and applicability of the hegemonic version was also examined. When all nations in the system pursued hegemonic policies, only two conditions were found for which all the theory's axioms held. These conditions were also rather stringent in their requirements for the power relationships between opposing and neutral actors. Although these conditions were restrictive and few in number, their existence demonstrated that this version of the theory was logically consistent.

The hegemonic version was then modified by allowing some nations in the system to pursue equality policies. We found that the number of conditions identifying the theory's applicability increased from two to four. Therefore, the hegemonic version had greater applicability once we permitted some nations in the system to pursue equality policies.

Chapters 3 and 4 concerned the consistency and applicability of the different versions of the balance of power theory. Determining the consistency and applicability of the theory involved analyses of the theory's axioms.

5

THE CONSEQUENCES OF THE BALANCE
OF POWER THEORY

This chapter examines a third critical characteristic of the theory—soundness (or validity). A theory is sound if its consequences are logically implied by its axioms. If a theory is sound, the axioms of the theory provide an explanation for its consequences. (This kind of explanation is a necessary ingredient of any theory that purports to be scientific.)

Several contradictory views are expressed in the literature concerning the theory's consequences. For example, some writers argue that the resulting power distribution between the system's opposing actors is equal; others argue that it is unequal. One possible explanation for this is that the axioms of the theory are inconsistent and consequently imply contradictory statements (see chapter 1). The analyses of chapters 3 and 4, however, demonstrate that the axioms of each version of the theory are consistent. I therefore turn to another property—soundness—in an attempt to explain and resolve these contradictory claims. Because I have also specified the applicability of the theory, an examination of soundness can now tell us which of the conflicting claims is valid, or whether both claims are valid under different sets of conditions.

A review of the literature indicates that at least three consequences are claimed for the theory—the resulting power distribution between opposing actors, the occurrence of war, and the survival of independent nations. There are conflicting claims concerning the first two consequences but general agreement on the third. First I review the literature that describes these consequences. I then discuss what my analysis indicates with regard to these contradictions.

Note that the relationship between the theory and two of its reputed consequences—the occurrence of war and the survival of independent nations—are treated as additional assumptions (or axioms) of the theory in order to determine the validity of the conflicting claims concerning the occurrence of war and to specify the conditions necessary for protecting the independence of nations.

Let me illustrate the necessity for doing this by considering the following argument:

Axiom 1: All people who smoke die of cancer.

Axiom 2: X smokes if X is under stress.

Conclusion: X's propensity for a heart attack increases. Note that in axiom (2), X's being under stress is a condition or value that makes the claim—X smokes—a valid claim. Note, too, that the conclusion is not valid. Suppose, however, that medical research has established that people who smoke have an increased propensity for heart attacks. If we treat this statement as an additional assumption, and if we find that X is under stress (i.e., the condition that allows us to conclude that X smokes), we can conclude that X's propensity for a heart attack increases.

We treat the consequences concerning war and national survival in an analogous manner. Balance of power writers establish a relationship between components of the theory and these consequences. By treating these relationships as additional assumptions in our model, we can draw upon the results of the analyses of chapters 3 and 4 to resolve the conflicting claims concerning the occurrence of war and to specify the conditions for national survival.

This point should become clear when we examine each of the consequences of the resulting power distribution between opponents:

RESULTING POWER DISTRIBUTION
BETWEEN OPPOSING ACTORS

While writers agree that the resulting power distribution is a major consequence of the theory, they disagree on what that distribution is. One group claims that the theory implies equal power distributions between opposing actors while another claims that the theory implies unequal power distributions.

In one of the earlier expositions of the balance of power theory, Machiavelli (n.d.:329) and Sir Thomas Overbury (1903:227) describe the theory as having "an inherent tendency to form *even power distributions* between contending actors." More recently, Butterfield describes the theory in the following terms:

> The whole order of Europe was a kind of terrestrial counterpart of the Newtonian system of astronomy . . . when one of these bodies increased its mass, the rest could recover an equilibrium [i.e., equal distribution of power] only by regrouping themselves, like a set of ballet dancers, making a necessary

rectification in the distances and producing new combinations (Butterfield, 1966:142).

In another study, Schwarzenberger (1941:117-18) claims that "the grouping of nations into alliances and counteralliances *produced an equal distribution of power* between these forces. . . . " and concludes by describing this power distribution as "an historical truism." One of the theory's most ardent proponents, Hans J. Morgenthau (1973:4-14), argues that *an equal distribution of power is inevitable* if nations abide by the principles of "political realism;" that is, they pursue their interests, which are defined in terms of power. Wolfers argues that

> . . . if one may assume that any government in its senses will be deeply concerned with the relative power position of hostile countries, then one may conclude that efforts to keep in step in the competition for power with such opponents, or even to outdo them, will almost certainly be forthcoming. If most nations react in this way, a *tendency towards an equilibrium* [italics mine] [that is, an equal distribution of power] will follow . . . forces appear to be working . . . pushing them in the direction of balanced power (Wolfers, 1962:123).

In his literature review, Claude (1967:51) concludes that most theorists consider the theory a means of *producing an equal distribution of power* between contending actors.

On the other hand, some writers claim that the theory is a means of producing unequal power distributions between the system's opposing actors. Organski asserts that when

> . . . we look at the whole sweep of history, for the past 150 years, we find that *equal power distributions are the exception, not the rule* . . . a more accurate view of the distribution of power in the years 1815-1914 finds England the senior partner in a *combination of overwhelming* [italics mine] power, supported at the beginning of the period by the second most powerful nation of Europe and underwritten at the end of the period by the growing giant that was soon to take her place (Organski, 1958:291-93).

Spykman (1942:105) describes Great Britain's role in the balance of power system as one that produced a *preponderance of power* in which "a divided Europe meant British hegemony." Nicholson (1942:123), too, describes the period of 1814-1914 as a "century of *British supremacy*," where Britain was "strong enough to discourage aggression in others and vulnerable enough not to practice aggression herself."

We turn now to the analyses of chapters 3 and 4 in respect to these contradictory claims.

69

Results of Analysis with Respect to Power Distribution

In two of the three versions, both claims concerning power distribution are valid. Specifically, equal and unequal power distributions are implied by the axioms of the balancer and equality versions of the theory. On the other hand, there is only one valid claim in the hegemonic version; namely, that the resulting power distribution between opponents is equal (see chapter 4, section III). If some nations ($< n/2$) are allowed to pursue equality policies, however, unequal power distributions are also implied in the hegemonic version. (See chapter 4, section IV.)

Let us examine each of the versions more closely to see what conditions (or assumptions) imply these consequences. In the balancer version, equal power distributions are implied by the fixed axioms and one of the following assumptions (or conditions):

1. The power of the opposing alliances is equal and the balancer nation pursues an equality policy (Table 3);

2. The power of the opposing alliances is equal and the balancer pursues a hegemonic policy and its power is greater than the power of each alliance (Table 3);

3. The power of the opposing alliances is unequal, the balancer nation pursues an equality policy and its power is equal to the difference in power between the opposing alliances (Table 4);

4. The power of the opposing alliances is unequal, the stronger alliance pursues a hegemonic policy, the balancer pursues a hegemonic policy, its power is equal to the difference in power between the opposing alliances, and it is more powerful than the weaker alliance (Table 4, cases 7 and 8);

5. The power of the opposing alliances is unequal, the more powerful alliance pursues an equality policy, and the power of the balancer is equal to the difference in power between the opposing alliances (Table 4, cases 4 and 6).

On the other hand, we find that an *unequal power distribution* results between opposing alliances in the balancer version when the power of the opposing alliances is unequal and:

1. Both the balancer and the more powerful alliance pursue equality policies and the power of the balancer is greater than or equal to twice the difference in power between the opposing alliances (Table 4, cases 1 and 3);

2. The balancer pursues a hegemonic policy, its power is greater than or equal to twice the difference in power between opposing alliances, and the more powerful alliance pursues an equality policy (Table 4, case 4);

70

3. The balancer pursues a hegemonic policy, it is stronger than the more powerful alliance, and the more powerful alliance pursues an equality policy (Table 4, case 6).

Turning to the equality version, we find that an *equal power distribution* is implied by the fixed axioms and the following assumption:

> There is a nation in the system whose power is equal to the difference in power between the opposing nations or the alliances that form. (See chapter 4, section I.)

On the other hand, an *unequal power distribution* results between opposing actors (nations or alliances) in the equality version when the power of opposing actors is unequal, no nation in the system satisfies the condition for equality, and there is a nation in the system whose power is greater than or equal to twice the difference in power between the opposing actors. (See chapter 4, section I.)

Examining the results obtained in the analysis of the hegemonic version, we find that *equal power distributions* are implied by the fixed axioms under the following conditions:

> 1. There is a nation in the system whose power is equal to the difference in power between opposing actors and is more powerful than the weaker actor, and the power of all other nations in the system is greater than the power of the alliances. (See chapter 4, section III.)
>
> 2. There is a nation in the system whose power is equal to the difference in power between opposing actors, and whose power is less than or equal to the power of the weaker actor, and this nation allies with the weaker actor. Additionally, the power of all other nations in the system is greater than the power of the alliances. (See chapter 4, section III.)

The results of the analysis in chapter 4, section III, indicate, however, that *unequal power distributions* are not implied by the fixed axioms under any set of conditions. Consequently, the claim that unequal power distributions between opponents result in systems where all nations pursue hegemonic policies is not valid.

To recapitulate, the analyses of chapters 3 and 4 indicate that the contradictory claims concerning the resulting power distribution between opponents are both valid. Specifically, both claims are valid in the equality and balancer versions of the theory under different sets of conditions. These conditions, in turn, specify the policy objectives of actors in the system, and the power relationships between opposing and neutral actors; in conjunction with the fixed axioms, they logically imply equal and unequal power distributions. Note that if writers had initially specified these conditions, the claims made with regard to the resulting power distribution would not have appeared to be contradictory.

OCCURRENCE OF WAR

Most writers agree that the occurrence of war is a major consequence of the theory. They disagree, however, on what power distribution between opponents contributes to war. Those who claim that equal power distributions are a consequence of the theory believe that equal power distributions contribute to the likelihood of peace; because neither opponent is assured of victory, neither initiates war. On the other hand, when the power distribution is unequal, the more powerful opponent, assured of victory, does not hesitate to initiate war. Claude finds that the majority of writers believe that the balance of power system promotes peace because the system produces an equal distribution of power between opponents:

> Some may choose to call equilibrium [i.e., an equal distribution of power] a safeguard of independence, or a barrier to universal empire, or the foundation of stability, abjuring all talk of peace. However, in so doing, they are really implying that the existence of equilibrium tends to promote peace—it protects the independence of states by discouraging disturbances. The sober recognition that deterrence may fail is quite compatible with all of this, but the point is that all the merits which are ascribed to equilibrium involve the claim, admittedly or not, that it contributes to the likelihood of peace (Claude, 1967:55).

On the other hand, another group of writers believes that unequal power distributions further the likelihood of peace. Not surprisingly, this is the same group who argue that unequal power distributions between opponents are consequences of the theory. They believe that an unequal power distribution (or preponderance) promotes peace because the more powerful opponent has no need to go to war, while the weaker side would be foolish to do so. They also believe that an equal power distribution between opponents increases the likelihood of war because each opponent thinks it can win. Pollard (1923:63), for example, argues that "in a simple balance the two scales must be nearly even, and the more perfect the balance the more easily it is upset. . . ." He further adds, *"we shall get no peace from a balance of power* [that is, an equal distribution of power] *."*

Nicholson agrees:

> If the balance [that is, preponderance] of power were concentrated in the hands of peace-loving nations, and if the rest of the world were convinced that if danger arose, that power would be jointly exercised to enforce peace, then wars would not arise (Nicholson, 1960:33).

Organski asserts that

> . . . the relationship between peace and the balance of power [that is, an equal distribution of power] appears to be exactly the opposite of what has been claimed. The periods of balance [equality], real or imagined, are periods of warfare, while the periods of known preponderance are periods of peace (Organski, 1958:292).

Analyses and Their Implications for Peace

A balance of power system produces either equal or unequal power distributions, which in turn contribute to the probability that the system is peaceful. Since equal and unequal power distributions are both valid consequences of the theory, the conflicting claims concerning the likelihood of peace (or the occurrence of war) are also valid. Specifically, the conditions that imply that the resulting power distribution is equal are also the conditions that increase the likelihood of peace (or, alternatively, decrease the likelihood of war). Similarly, the conditions that imply unequal power distributions are also the conditions that increase the chances for peace. In other words, the system has a greater likelihood of being peaceful under the different sets of conditions that imply equal or unequal power distributions between opponents. Consequently, the conflicting claims concerning the likelihood of peace are both valid.

Note that in those situations where unequal power distributions contribute to the likelihood of peace, the more powerful alliance pursues an equality policy. This result supports the belief that "the danger presented by a dominant actor is directly proportionate to the degree of its power and efficiency *and* to the *spontaneity or 'inevitableness' of its ambitions"* (Butterfield, 1953:66). Claude (1967:66) made this point most simply when he wrote, "preponderance may serve [peace] if the *right state(s)* is master of the situation."

SURVIVAL OF INDEPENDENT NATIONS

Unlike the former consequences, most balance of power theorists agree that the preservation (or survival) of nations is a major consequence of the theory. Butterfield (1966:142) remarks that the balance of power system was the only system "which made it possible for a considerable number of states to remain in existence at all." In another study, Morgenthau (1973: 176-77) claims that "small states have always owed their existence to the balance of power." Herz (1969:64), comparing the balance of power system of the nineteenth century with the contemporary international system, finds that the balance of power system "afforded small states protection."

The general argument supporting this claim is that the independence of nations is protected as long as neutral nations behave in a manner consistent with axiom (2). That is, independence is safeguarded if neutral nations come to the assistance of weaker actors when the latter are threatened by more powerful and aggressive opponents. Gulick, for example, argues that

> . . . if one granted that the survival of independent states was the primary aim and added that the best chance of achieving it resided in preserving the state system, a relentless logic led to the obvious axiom of preventing the preponderance of any one member of the state system (Gulick, 1955:33-34).

In a similar argument, Gooch claims that the balance of power system

> . . . is the determination, partly curious and partly instinctive, to resist by diplomacy or arms the growth of any European state or coalition at once so formidable and so actually or potentially hostile as to threaten our liberties, the security of our shores, the safety of our commerce or the integrity of our foreign affairs (Gooch, 1939:78).

Schwarzenberger (1941:122) exhorts nations to prevent the emergence of dominant actors and in fact asserts that "the balance of power system in Europe means in effect the independence of several states; the preponderance of any one power threatens and destroys this independence."

Haas finds that

> . . . historically the balance of power has been held out as a means of planning policy in an intelligent and dispassionate manner by setting forth operational rules whereby the survival of single states within the system might be assured (Haas, 1953a:371).

The operational rules to which Haas refers are, in effect, stated in axiom (2). As long as nations use axiom (2) as a policy guide by preventing the emergence of dominant and power-hungry actors, their independence and the independence of weaker actors is protected.

Briefly, when nations act in accordance with axiom (2), their independence is safeguarded. On the other hand, if axiom (2) is not satisfied, their independence is imperiled. Let us turn now to the analyses of chapters 3 and 4 to see what they indicate regarding this claim.

Analyses and Their Implications for the Independence of Nations

Whenever axiom (2) is not satisfied, the independence of nations is uncertain. The results in Tables 3 and 4 indicate that the policy pursued by the balancer nation affects the survivability of nations in the system. This is because the number of conditions for which axiom (2) does not hold is greater when the balancer pursues a hegemonic policy than when the balancer pursues an equality policy. Additionally, when the balancer pursues a hegemonic policy, it allies with the more powerful opponent; where it pursues an equality policy and axiom (2) is not satisfied, the balancer remains neutral. We can therefore conclude that when the balancer nation pursues an equality policy, nations in the system have better chances of surviving as independent units. The belief that the balancer "must be somewhat different from other nations . . . in using its power only to maintain a balance [i.e., equality] " (Organski, 1958:286) receives support when we consider violations of axiom (2) and their implications for the survival of independent nations.

Turning to the results of the equality version, we find that axiom (2) is always satisfied, and the independence of nations in the system is therefore protected. In systems where all nations pursue policies aimed at equalizing the power difference of opposing actors, nations in the system are assured survival.

On the other hand, in systems where the policies of opposing and neutral nations are aimed at improving their respective power relationships, national survival is most precarious. (See chapter 4, section III.) The survival of independent nations is in great danger in this system because axiom (2) is violated in all but two configurations of power relationships between opposing and neutral actors. (See Table 5 and conditions (1) and (2), chapter 4, section III.)

National independence, then, is protected when axiom (2) is satisfied. A more specific form of this argument is Morgenthau's (1973:168-71) belief that the balance of power system safeguards the independence of nations. Morgenthau, a leading proponent of the balance of power theory, assumes that there is a system with three nations—A, B and C—that satisfy the following power relationships: A=B and A > C. He further assumes that A has hegemonic ambitions and threatens to dominate C, and that nation B favors the status quo. He then concludes that B allies with C to prevent A from overtaking C. Because B allies with C, C's independence is secure.

In terms of our model, A assumes the role of a_i, B assumes the role of a_j and C assumes the role of a_{-i}. Consequently, the power relationships are: $k_i = k_j$ and $k_i > k_{-i}$. Nation a_i (A) is assumed to pursue a hegemonic policy, nation a_j (B) an equality policy and a_{-i} (C) an equality policy. Since the power of A and B are assumed to be equal, it seems justifiable to assume that B pursues an equality policy in trying to maintain the status quo. Regarding C's foreign policy, it is not clear from Morgenthau's argument whether C desires to maintain the status quo or desires a change in the existing power relationship. However, our analysis provides the same results whether C is assumed to pursue an equality or a hegemonic policy.

Briefly then, the assumptions are:

1. a_i pursues a hegemonic policy;
2. a_j, a_{-i} pursue equality policies;
3. $k_i = k_j$;
4. $k_i > k_{-i}$.

Assumption (3) implies that $k_j > d$ (where $d = k - k_{-i}$). We now determine under what conditions a_j allies with a_{-i}. We must consider the following cases because a_j pursues an equality policy and seeks to minimize $|d|$. (a) $k_j \geqslant 2d$ and (b) $k_j < 2d$.

a. $k_j \geqslant 2d$
   $k_j \geqslant 2(k_j - k_{-i})$
   $k_j/2 \geqslant k_j - k_{-i}$
   $k_j \leqslant 2k_{-i}$

b. $k_j < 2d$
   $k_j < 2(k_j - k_{-i})$
   $-k_j/2 < -k_{-i}$
   $k_j > 2k_{-i}$

In (a) where $k_j \leqslant 2k_{-i}$, a_j does not ally with a_{-i}. But in (b) where $k_j > 2k_{-i}$, a_j allies with a_{-i} and according to Morgenthau's claim, safeguards the independence of a_{-i}. This analysis demonstrates, however, that the independence of all nations is not protected. Axiom (2) is not satisfied when the power of a_j is less than or equal to twice the power of the weaker nation (condition [a]). The uncommitted nation, a_j, comes to the aid of the weaker opponent, a_{-i}, only when its power is greater than twice the power of the weaker opponent (condition [b]). This analysis also demonstrates that the independence of relatively weak nations in the system is safeguarded. Morgenthau's (1973:176-77) conclusion that "small states have always owed their independence either to the balance of power [i.e., an equal power distribution] or to the preponderance of one protecting power," is supported here. On the other hand, Morgenthau's argument also reveals that the independence of major nations in the system is not protected.

SUMMARY

This chapter examined the validity of three conflicting consequences claimed for the balance of power theory—the resulting power distribution between opposing actors, the occurrence of war, and the preservation of independent nations.

We found that in the equality and balancer versions, the contradictory claims concerning the resulting power distribution were both validated under different sets of conditions. On the other hand, an unequal power distribution was not a valid claim when all nations in the system pursued hegemonic policies.

We also found that the conflicting claims concerning the occurrence of war were valid. As was the case with the resulting power distribution, the contradictory claims regarding peace were valid under different sets of conditions. The contradictory claims present in the literature, then, were only apparent contradictions, not real ones.

We also examined the relationship between the theory's axioms and the consequence—preservation of independent nations. Most writers agreed that insofar as axiom (2) was satisfied, the independence of nations was preserved. We therefore examined the cases in which axiom (2) was not satisfied to see when national survival was endangered. We found that when all nations in the system pursued equality policies, national survival was always assured. On the other hand, when all nations in the system pursued hegemonic policies, we found that national survival was precarious except under two fairly restrictive sets of conditions. Regarding the balancer version, we found that the nations in the system had better chances of surviving as independent nations if the balancer pursued an equality policy than if the balancer pursued a hegemonic policy.

At this point, we have only considered systems in which the initial power distribution is unequal. Some writers, however, assume that the nations in a balance of power system have equal amounts of power. Chapter 6 analyzes the consistency, soundness and applicability of the theory where we assume that this is so.

6

ANALYSIS OF APPLICABILITY AND SOUNDNESS WHEN THE INITIAL POWER DISTRIBUTION IS EQUAL

In the analyses of chapters 3 and 4 we noted that the only restriction most writers impose on the initial distribution of power in a balance of power system is the absence of a dominant actor (i.e., axiom [1]). However, there is a group of writers who impose additional restrictions on the initial power distribution; specifically, that nations in the system have comparable or equal amounts of power. Kulski (1964:11-12) claims that "there must exist a multistate international stage shared by great powers of roughly comparable strength." In addition, "the system requires for its operation a slow rate of change in the distribution of power," in order to maintain power parity. This assumption is viewed by Kulski as one of the conditions necessary for satisfying the theory's axioms.

The general claim seems to be that when the distribution of power among nations is equal, the balance of power theory is applicable. There is disagreement, however, concerning the effect of the number of actors of equal strength on the applicability of the theory. Kulski (1964:11) claims that three or more nations of comparable strength are necessary for satisfying the axioms of the theory. Herz (1959:65) claims that a balance of power system must contain a "considerable number of 'big powers' not too dissimilar from each other and not too distant in power from lesser ones." Hoffman (1972:620) argues that the theory "requires a number of major actors, usually around five or six, of comparable, if not equal power" to be applicable. In fact, a debate has grown out of this ambiguity regarding the number of actors necessary for satisfying the axioms of the theory. Kaplan (1957b:22-36; 1969:292-96) and Morgenthau (1951:46-47) claim that as the number of actors of equal strength increases, applicability increases. They argue that a greater number of equal actors in the system increases the number of alliances that can occur, which in turn increases the possibilities of counterbalancing any preponderant state or alliance.

79

Kaplan (1957b:34) argues that "if there are only three actors who are relatively equal in power, the probability that two will combine to eliminate the third is great." He concludes that five is the minimum number of nations necessary to satisfy the axioms of the theory (Kaplan, et al., 1960: 245).

On the other hand, Waltz (1964, 1967) and Yalem (1972), among others (Liska, 1957; Wolfers, 1962; Aron, 1960), claim that an increase in the number of actors decreases applicability. These writers argue that a greater number of actors in the system increases the number of alliances that can occur, which in turn increases the possibilities for violating the axioms of the theory. Consequently, applicability increases as the number of actors of comparable power decreases.

This chapter examines the applicability and soundness of the balance of power theory when the initial distribution of power is equal. Chapters 3 and 4 have already demonstrated the consistency of each version of the theory. In our examination of these two properties, we address two questions:

First, what effect does the number of nations in the system have on the applicability of the theory? To answer this question, we examine the applicability of the theory in three-, four-, five- and six-nation systems. By varying the size of the system, we are able to determine if the applicability of the theory increases when we increase the number of nations in the system or when we decrease the number of nations in the system.

Second, what effect does the assumption of power parity have on the soundness of the theory? Because we must examine the applicability of the theory in order to examine soundness (chapter 1), we must first specify the applicability of the different versions of the theory to determine which of the conflicting claims concerning the theory's consequences is valid.

Since we are assuming that the initial power distribution is equal, the following analysis differs considerably from the analyses of chapters 3 and 4. Moreover, because we want to examine a relationship not examined previously—the relationship between the size of the system and the applicability of the theory—we have to make an assumption not made in the previous analyses.

When we examined systems with initially unequal distributions of power (chapters 3 and 4), we could infer that in at least one pair of nations, one was more powerful than the other. We referred to this pair as the system's opposing nations and began our analyses with the condition that the more powerful nation (or alliance) threatened its weaker opponent. This condition enabled us to study the dynamics of alliance formation; without it we would not have been able to determine under what conditions the theory was consistent and applicable. (See axiom [2] , chapter 2.)

In the following analysis, however, we cannot identify either of the opposing nations by the difference in their power. We therefore employ the following criterion (or condition) for identifying the systems's opposing nations.

Condition of Analysis

Any nation that pursues a *hegemonic* policy may oppose any other nation in the system.

This condition identifies the nation initiating the threat (i.e., the intimidating nation). Note that any nation that pursues a hegemonic policy can be the intimidating nation. Consequently, if a_1, a_2 and a_3 are in a three-nation system, and both a_1 and a_2 pursue hegemonic policies, we must consider the following cases: (1) a_1 opposes a_2, (2) a_1 opposes a_3, (3) a_2 opposes a_1, and (4) a_2 opposes a_3. Note, too, how this contrasts with the condition of the analyses in chapters 3 and 4 where we only had to consider the case of one intimidating nation in the system.

This condition also identifies the target nation, which can be any other nation in the system. In the previous analyses, the target nation is identified by its relative power position to the intimidating nation. Since we have no criterion for choosing any particular nation as a target, all nations are possible targets. Consequently, if a_1, a_2 and a_3 are the nations in a three-nation system, and a_1 pursues a hegemonic policy, we must consider the case where a_1 opposes a_2 and the case where a_1 opposes a_3. Note the contrast with the condition of the previous analyses where only one target nation in the system was considered a possibility.

Briefly, this condition identifies the dyad of opposing nations in systems with initially equal distributions of power. The intimidating nation is any nation that pursues a hegemonic policy, and the target nation is any other nation in the system, regardless of the policy it pursues.

The condition is necessary to our analysis because we are examining systems with initial power distributions that are different from those examined in chapters 3 and 4. In addition, we want specifically to determine how the number of nations in the system effect the applicability of the theory. Recall that one group of writers argues that applicability increases as the number of nations increases, while another argues that applicability decreases as the number of nations increases.

Let us digress for a moment. Suppose we have a six-nation system in which one nation, say, a_1, pursues a hegemonic policy. According to the condition above, we must consider five possibilities: (1) a_1 opposes a_2, (2) a_1 opposes a_3, (3) a_1 opposes a_4, (4) a_1 opposes a_5, and (5) a_1 opposes a_6. Suppose further that in all five cases the theory is applicable. In the real world, however, nations are distinct units. If one nation in a six-nation system pursues a hegemonic policy, it could be any one of the six (a_1, a_2, a_3, a_4, a_5 or a_6). So instead of claiming only five cases, we should claim thirty (6 possible intimidating nations x 5 possible target nations).

Clearly, then, the number of cases (or possibilities) in which the theory is applicable (or inapplicable) increases when nations become distinct units. In order to more accurately evaluate the claims of both groups, we include in our analysis the additional cases that result from treating nations as distinct entities.

Assumption of This Analysis
A nation is equally likely to pursue a hegemonic or an equality policy.

This assumption preserves the identity of the nations in the system. It requires us to consider, for example, the case of one nation that pursues a hegemonic policy in a three-nation system, as six distinct cases (3 possible intimidating nations x 2 possible target nations).

Examining the relationship between the size of the system and the applicability of the theory has not only led to the above assumption, but has also directed the organization of our study toward the analysis of applicability according to the number of nations in the system. (The analyses of applicability in chapters 3 and 4 were organized according to the different versions of the theory.) Nevertheless, we can examine the applicability of the balancer version, for example, by reviewing all those cases in three-, four-, five- and six-nation systems where every nation except one (i.e., the balancer nation) has allied with one of the opposing alliances and the balancer pursues an equality policy (in accordance with axiom [4]). Similarly, we examine the applicability of the equality version by reviewing all those cases in three-, four-, five- and six-nation systems where the majority of nations in the system pursue equality policies (i.e., the nation acts in accordance with axiom [3] if it is a target and axiom [4] if it is a neutral nation). Finally, the cases of the hegemonic version include all those cases in three-, four-, five- and six-nation systems where the majority of nations pursue hegemonic policies (i.e., acts in accordance with axiom [3'] if it is one of the opposing nations and axiom [4'] if it is a neutral nation). In short, we analyze the same combinations of axioms as in chapters 3 and 4.

There are three major differences between the previous analyses of applicability and soundness and the following treatment. The first difference involves the condition used to identify the system's opposing nations: in the analyses of chapters 3 and 4 where the initial power distribution was unequal, opposing actors were identified by the difference in their power. For this analysis, the intimidating nation is identified by the policy objective it pursues and the target nation is any other nation in the system, whereas earlier analyses assumed that the more powerful nation (or alliance) was the intimidating actor and the weaker nation (or alliance) was the target. Second, in this analysis we specifically assume that all nations are equally likely to pursue equality or hegemonic policies. This enables us to preserve the identity of nations in the system. We can more accurately evaluate the effect that the size of the system has on the applicability of the theory when we preserve the identity of nations in the system. Finally, in the previous chapters we analyzed the applicability of each version of the theory separately, while here we analyze the applicability of the theory according to the size of the system. Having completed the analyses of three-, four-, five- and six-nation systems, we review those cases of the balancer, equality and hegemonic versions when we discuss the different versions.

ANALYSIS

If the system contains a nation, say a_1, with a hegemonic policy, a_1 may oppose any other nation in the system. It is therefore necessary to examine the applicability of the theory in the case when a_1 opposes a_2, when a_1 opposes a_3, and so on. The additional assumption in this analysis says that any nation is equally likely to pursue a hegemonic or equality policy. It is necessary, then, to examine the applicability of the theory when a_2 opposes a_1, a_2 opposes a_3, and so on. To study the theory's applicability and soundness, it is therefore necessary to examine the mutual satisfiability of axioms (1), (2), (3), (3'), (4) and (4') in each case for three-, four-, five- and six-nation systems.

In a three-nation system, the following situations have to be considered: no nation pursues a hegemonic policy, one nation pursues a hegemonic policy, two nations pursue hegemonic policies, and three nations pursue hegemonic policies.

In the first situation, only one case is examined since there are no opposing actors in the system. However, six cases are considered when one nation in the system pursues a hegemonic policy. Either a_1, a_2 or a_3 may pursue hegemonic policies. Furthermore, if a_1 (a_2 or a_3) pursues a hegemonic policy, a_1 may oppose a_2 (a_1 or a_3) or a_3 (a_1 or a_2). If two nations in the system pursue hegemonic policies, twelve cases are examined. Either a_1 and a_2, a_2 and a_3, a_1 and a_3 pursue hegemonic policies while a_3, a_1, a_2 pursue equality policies, respectively. If, for example, a_1 and a_2 pursue hegemonic policies, a_1 may oppose a_2 or a_3, or a_2 may oppose a_1 or a_3. Four cases are therefore examined when a_1 and a_2 pursue hegemonic policies: (1) a_1 opposes a_2; (2) a_1 opposes a_3; (3) a_2 opposes a_1; (4) a_2 opposes a_3. Similarly, four cases are examined when a_2 and a_3 pursue hegemonic policies, and when a_1 and a_3 pursue hegemonic policies. Finally, six cases are examined when all nations in the system pursue hegemonic policies: a_1 may oppose a_2 or a_3 ; a_2 may oppose a_1 or a_3 ; and a_3 may oppose a_1 or a_2. Thus, a total of twenty-five cases are examined in a three-nation system.

In a similar manner 97 cases are examined in four-nation systems, 321 cases in five-nation systems, and 961 cases in six-nation systems. (See appendix C for the analyses of three-, four- and five-nation systems.)

FINDINGS

The Effect of Size of System on the Applicability of the Theory

The proportion of cases in which the axioms of the theory are not simultaneously satisfied is tabulated in Table 6. Clearly, as the number of nations increases, the possibilities for aligning and opposing other members in the system increases. The results compiled in Table 6 indicate that the proportion of cases in which the axioms of the theory are simultaneously satisfied does not increase as the size of the system increases. Table 6 indicates that five-nation systems yield as many or fewer cases that satisfy the axioms of the theory than do three- and four-nation systems. As a result, this analysis refutes the claims of Kaplan (1957b) and others that larger systems increase the applicability of the theory, due to an increase in the number of possible alliance formations.

The claim that applicability increases as the number of nations in the system decreases, is not supported by this analysis. Table 6 indicates that the theory is inapplicable in a greater proportion of cases in three-nation systems than in six-nation systems.

Briefly, this analysis demonstrates that neither of the conflicting claims concerning the relationship between system size and the theory's applicability is valid. A recent study by Ostrom and Aldrich (1978) supports this conclusion. Surprisingly, however, Table 6 indicates that when the number of nations in the system is even, applicability is considerably greater than when the number is uneven. For four- and six-nation systems, the proportion of cases in which the axioms of the theory are satisfied is greater than two-thirds. On the other hand, in three- and five-nation systems, the proportion of cases in which the axioms are satisfied is approximately one-half. We note that writers do not always distinguish between even and uneven numbers of nations.

Applicability of the Different Versions of the Theory

Balancer version. In this version of the theory at least one nation in the role of balancer must pursue an equality policy. Kulski (1964:12) argues that the minimal condition for satisfying axioms (1) and (2) is that "at least one great power of considerable strength remain uncomitted and the others

84

TABLE 6
PROPORTION OF CASES IN WHICH BALANCE
OF POWER THEORY IS INAPPLICABLE

Number of Nations in System	Number of Inapplicable Cases	Proportion of Inapplicable Cases	Proportion of Applicable Cases
3 nations	12	12/25, $\approx 1/2$	1/2
4 nations	24	24/97, $< 1/4$	3/4
5 nations	160	160/321, $\approx 1/2$	1/2
6 nations	300	300/961, $< 1/3$	2/3

be kept in line by the potential sanction of its throwing its weight on the scale of the weaker side against the stronger." Herz claims that a

> . . . balance of power system was rendered possible partly by the existence of one insular power . . . who would intervene as "holder of the balance" whenever the equilibrium was endangered by the expansionist policies of a would-be hegemonic power (Herz, 1959:65).

It is interesting to note that applicability of the balancer version changes as the size of the system changes. Specifically, in three- and four-nation systems, when the majority of nations pursue hegemonic policies, this version is applicable in every case. For example, in a three-nation system, when one hegemonic nation threatens another hegemonic nation, the balancer remains neutral and all the axioms are satisfied. In a four-nation system, the balancer nation allies with the weaker side when two hegemonic nations oppose a third hegemonic nation and all the axioms are simultaneously satisfied.

However, when the *number of nations is greater than four*, and the *majority pursue hegemonic policies*, the theory is not applicable in every case. For example, in a five-nation system, if three nations pursue hegemonic policies and two pursue equality policies, the theory is inapplicable whenever one of the equality-oriented nations is the target nation. Additionally, when four nations in a five-nation system pursue hegemonic policies, three hegemonic nations oppose the remaining hegemonic nation; although the balancer acts in a manner consistent with axiom (2) and allies with the weaker side, axiom (1) is not satisfied. Similarly, when five nations in a six-nation system pursue hegemonic policies, the balance of power theory is inapplicable. If one hegemonic nation threatens another hegemonic nation, the remaining hegemonic nations ally on the side of one opponent. Although the balancer comes to the aid of the weaker side, axiom (1) is nevertheless violated.

All (or most) nations pursue equality policies. When all nations in the system are equal in power and a majority pursue equality policies, the balance of power theory is *applicable in every case.* Furthermore, the theory's axioms are satisfied regardless of how many nations are in the system. Alliances occur only in systems with four or more nations. Whenever an alliance forms, a counterbalancing alliance forms in turn, and produces results consistent with the axioms of the theory. It is interesting to note that very few theorists describe the balance of power theory as one in which all nations in the system are equal in power and the majority pursue equality policies. Most theorists who argue that the initial distribution of power must be equal describe the nations as adopting hegemonic policies.

All (or most) nations pursue hegemonic policies. The hegemonic version is most prevalent among those who argue that the initial distribution of power is equal. In this version most, if not all, nations are seen as pursuing hegemonic policies. For example, Hoffman (1972:620) describes the nations in the system as "trying to maximize their power at each others' expense." Kaplan (1957b:22-34) and Morgenthau (1951:46-47), too, describe the international system as one in which "nations are equal in power and strive to increase their power to the detriment of the others."

This version is by far the most inapplicable version of the theory. It is the most inapplicable because, in a large proportion of cases, the alliances and counteralliances that form do not satisfy the axioms of the theory. Table 7 lists the proportion of cases in which the hegemonic version is inapplicable, for three-, four-, five- and six-nation systems.

As Table 7 indicates, when a majority of nations in a three-nation system pursue hegemonic policies, the theory is inapplicable in two-thirds of the cases (i.e., in twelve out of eighteen cases). In a four-nation system, it is inapplicable for one-half of them. In a five-nation system, when three, four and five nations pursue hegemonic policies, the theory is inapplicable for 160/221, or 8/11 of the cases considered. Finally, in a six-nation system, when four, five and six nations pursue hegemonic policies, the theory is inapplicable in 300/480 or 5/8 of the cases examined. Regardless of the size of the system, the proportion of cases in which the theory's axioms are not simultaneously satisfied increases as the number of nations pursuing hegemonic policies increases.

To recapitulate, this analysis demonstrates that the applicability of the theory is different in each version. When a majority of nations of equal power pursue *equality* policies, the theory is applicable in every case,

TABLE 7
HEGEMONIC VERSION – MAJORITY OF NATIONS
PURSUING HEGEMONIC POLICIES

Number of Nations	Theory Is Inapplicable
3-nation system	2/3 of the cases
4-nation system	1/2 of the cases
5-nation system	8/11 of the cases
6-nation system	5/8 of the cases

regardless of the number of nations in the system. When a majority of nations of equal power pursue *hegemonic* policies, the theory is inapplicable in at least half of the cases examined, regardless of the number of nations in the system. On the other hand, the number of nations in the system does affect the applicability of the balancer version; one nation in a balancer position that pursues an equality policy is viewed as crucial to satisfying the theory's axioms. In three- and four-nation systems, the balancer version is applicable in every case. However, for larger systems, the presence of a balancer nation pursuing an equality policy does not guarantee the simultaneous satisfaction of the theory's axioms, and the theory is therefore not applicable in every case.

Soundness
A review of the literature in chapter 5 indicated that at least three consequences were claimed for the theory. They were the resulting power distribution between opposing actors, the occurrence of war, and the survival of independent nations. We now examine each of these consequences to determine if and when they are logically implied by the axioms of the theory (i.e., if they are sound).

Resulting Power Distribution Between Opposing Actors
We also noted in chapter 5 that while writers agree that the resulting power distribution is a major consequence of the theory, they disagree on what that distribution is. Specifically, one group of writers claims that the theory implies equal power distributions between opposing actors while another group claims that the theory implies unequal power distributions between opposing actors.

Our analysis indicates that when the initial distribution of power in the system is equal, *only equal* power distributions between opposing actors occur. If all nations in the system have equal amounts of power, the claims of those who assert that unequal power distributions are implied by the axioms of the theory are not valid.

The Occurrence of War

Most writers agree that the occurrence of war is a major consequence of the theory. They disagree, however, on what power distribution between opponents contributes to war. Specifically, some writers believe that equal power distributions between opposing actors contribute to the likelihood of peace (or alternatively, the absence of war) while others claim that unequal power distributions between opposing actors contribute to the likelihood of peace. (See chapter 5.)

Since we already noted that unequal power distributions between opposing actors do not occur in systems with initially equal power distributions, we conclude that the claim—unequal power distributions contribute to the likelihood of peace—is not valid. We can also conclude that systems in which the majority of nations pursue equality policies are systems with the greatest likelihood of peace because balance of power writers maintain that when the system produces equal power distributions between opposing actors, the likelihood of peace is high. In all cases where the majority of nations pursue equality policies, the system produces equal power distributions between opposing actors. Additionally, in systems with an even number of nations, the propensity for peace is high because the proportion of cases in which equal power distributions are produced is approximately 75% (73/97) in four-nation systems and 67% (661/961) in six-nation systems.

On the other hand, the likelihood of peace is relatively low in systems where the majority of nations pursue hegemonic policies. When the majority pursue hegemonic policies, the proportion of cases in which equal power distributions result between opposing actors is never more than 50% (Table 7). Further, the likelihood of peace is relatively low in systems with an uneven number of nations; equal power distributions between opposing actors occur in only 50% of the cases examined (Table 6).

Survival of Independent Nations

Many writers claim that the survival of independent nations is another consequence of the balance of power theory. The general argument is that, to the extent that neutral nations behave in a manner consistent with axiom (2), the survival of nations in the system is assured: in other words, that nations are guaranteed their survival if axiom (2) is satisfied. (See chapter 5.)

This study indicates that a nation is assured of its survival if a neutral nation pursues an equality policy. When this is the case, the neutral nation comes to the aid of the weaker side, and axiom (2) is satisfied. However, if the neutral nation pursues a hegemonic policy, the survival of weaker nation(s) is not guaranteed. In this case, the neutral nation always allies with the more preponderant actor. The assurance of national survival, then, is dependent upon the policy objectives pursued by neutral nations.

SUMMARY

In this chapter we examined the applicability and soundness of the balance of power theory when the initial power distribution among nations in the system was assumed to be equal. Specifically, we examined the effect that the size of the system had on the applicability of the theory, as well as the applicability and soundness of each version under this initial condition of power parity.

We examined the applicability of the theory in three-, four-, five- and six-nation systems. No support was found for the claim that an increase in the number of actors increases the applicability of the theory. Furthermore, no support was found for the claim that a decrease in the number of actors in the system increases the theory's applicability. Rather surprisingly, we found that even numbers of actors of equal strength satisfied the theory's axioms in a greater proportion of cases than did systems with uneven numbers of actors of equal strength. The relationship between even versus uneven numbers of actors and the theory's applicability has never been discussed in the literature.

An examination of the applicability of the different versions of the theory led us to conclude that in systems where the majority of nations pursued equality policies, the theory was applicable in every conceivable case of alignment and opposition. We noted that few writers described the balance of power system as one in which all nations were equal in power and where the majority of nations pursued equality policies (equality version). However, under these conditions, the balance of power axioms were always satisfied, regardless of the number of nations in the system. It could be that few writers describe the theory as operating under these conditions because they appear to be somewhat unrealistic. Nevertheless, these were the only conditions under which the theory was always applicable.

We found that the applicability of the balancer version was more limited than that of the equality version. In three- and four-nation systems, the axioms of the balancer version were satisfied in every case. The applicability of the balancer version was, however, more restrictive in five- and six-nation systems. In these systems, attempts by some for preponderance were not thwarted and the axioms were therefore not simultaneously satisfied. This result could be viewed as adding support to Kaplan's (1957b:35) claim that larger systems are more tolerant of a balancer nation because the latter is less effective in thwarting the ambitions of other nations' bids for hegemony.

The applicability of the hegemonic version was found to be the most limited of the three versions we examined. This version of the theory was inapplicable in more than 50% of the cases. Additionally, as we increased the number of nations that pursued hegemonic policies, the applicability of the theory decreased. As we noted, this version of the theory is the one most often presented in conjunction with the conditions of power parity among nations.

We also examined the soundness of the theory; that is, the extent to which the consequences claimed for the theory are implied by the axioms of the theory. We found that only one of the contradictory claims concerning the resulting power distribution and the occurrence of war was valid. Specifically, we found that in systems where the initial distribution of power among nations was assumed to be equal, only equal power distributions resulted between the system's opposing actors. Moreover, we found that only equal power distributions between opposing actors increased the likelihood of peace.

Finally, in examining the consequence—survival of independent nations—we found that the survival of nations was assured only when a neutral nation pursued an equality policy, in the sense that the neutral nation allied with the weaker opponent. If the neutral nation pursued a hegemonic policy, it always allied with the more powerful opponent.

7

SUMMARY

This study extended previous efforts to resolve the contradictions in the literature concerning the consequences of the balance of power theory. To resolve these contradictory claims, I examined three properties of the theory—consistency, soundness and applicability. A theory is consistent if its axioms do not imply contradictory statements. If the balance of power theory was found to be inconsistent, then the conflicting claims could be explained by the fact that the theory's axioms were inconsistent. A theory is sound (or valid) if its consequences are logically implied by its axioms. Finally a theory's applicability is known once all the conditions that simultaneously satisfy the axioms of the theory are specified. By ascertaining the applicability of the balance of power theory, I could determine if only one or both of the conflicting claims were valid inferences under different sets of conditions.

To examine these properties, I needed a formal statement of the basic axioms and consequences of the balance of power theory. Since no precise statement exists, I distilled the axioms and consequences from the traditional balance of power literature, and found a consensus concerning two of the theory's axioms. There was, however, a lack of agreement on the remaining axioms, which involved the policy objectives of the nations and alliances in a balance of power system. Three different sets of axioms were identified. To acknowledge this disagreement, I treated each set of policy objectives and the two axioms on which there was agreement as a distinct version of the theory. As a result, I examined the consistency, soundness and applicability of three different versions of the balance of power theory.

A review of the literature also revealed that at least three consequences were claimed for the theory. Although most writers agreed that the resulting power distribution between competing actors was a major consequence, they did not agree on what that distribution was. Similarly, while most writers agreed that the occurrence of war was a major consequence, they did not agree on what distribution of power resulted in war. The only consequence on which there was little disagreement was the one involving the survival of independent nations. Most writers agreed that the balance of power theory had safeguarded the independence of the nations in the system.

In addition, I found a lack of agreement on the initial distribution of power. While some writers described it as one in which all nations in the system had equal or comparable amounts of power, other writers imposed no restrictions at all. I therefore examined the consistency, soundness and applicability of the different versions of the theory both for systems with initially unequal and equal power distributions.

For systems with initially unequal power distributions, I found that the conflicting claims regarding the theory's consequences were valid under different sets of conditions; specifically, that the claims concerning the resulting power distribution between opposing actors were both valid, but under different sets of conditions. Likewise, I found that the conflicting claims concerning the occurrence of war were logically implied by the axioms of the theory under different sets of conditions. I was also able to specify the conditions under which the independence of nations was safeguarded in a balance of power system. These conditions involved the policy objectives and power relationships of the nations and alliances in the system and were not specified in previous expositions of the balance of power theory.

For systems with initially equal power distributions, I found that only one of the contradictory claims concerning the resulting power distribution between opponents and the occurrence of war was valid. I found that only equal power distributions arose between opposing actors in systems where nations had equal amounts of power. Additionally, I found that only equal power distributions between opposing actors increased the system's propensity for peace. The analysis also indicated that the independence of nations in the system was protected as long as neutral nations pursued equality policies. When neutral nations pursued hegemonic policies, the analysis indicated that national independence was endangered.

In systems where nations have equal amounts of power, writers also disagree on the effect that the size of the system has on the applicability of the theory. Some writers argue that applicability of the theory increases when the number of nations in the system increases, while others believe that applicability decreases when the number of nations increases. By examining the relationship between size and applicability for three-, four-, five- and six-nation systems, I found that the size of the system did not have any effect on the applicability of the theory. I found, however, that the theory was applicable in a larger proportion of cases in systems with an even number of nations than in systems with an uneven number. Writers have not considered the effect of even versus uneven numbers of nations on the applicability of the theory. Furthermore, I found that the theory was more applicable in systems where the majority of nations pursued equality policies than in systems where the majority of nations pursued hegemonic policies. (This was also true for systems with initially unequal power distributions.) Again, the effect of different policy objectives on the applicability of the theory has not been considered in the balance of power literature.

This study, then, demonstrated that the balance of power theory is logically consistent, and specified the conditions under which its consequences are valid. Consistency, soundness and applicability were necessary tools for resolving the contradictions in the literature, but they were also important in their own right. It is necessary to demonstrate the consistency and soundness of a theory if it is to have any utility for explaining and predicting. In light of the significance of the balance of power theory and its relationship to the literature on deterrence and the balance of terror, it was necessary to demonstrate that the balance of power theory satisfied these properties.

APPENDIXES

APPENDIX A
BALANCER VERSION, $k(S_i) = k(S_{-i})$

Case 3. S_i and S_{-i} pursue *hegemonic* policies (both act in accordance with axiom [3'] and a_j pursues an *equality* policy, axiom [4]). The theory is applicable if axioms (1), (2), (3') and (4) are simultaneously satisfied.

Both S_i and S_{-i} prefer to admit a_j as a member of their alliance since each wishes to increase D in its favor (according to axiom [3']). However, a_j prefers to remain neutral since $|D| = 0$ and u_j is maximized (according to axiom [4]). All the axioms are satisfied and the theory is applicable.

Case 4. S_i and S_{-i} pursue *equality* policies (both act in accordance with axiom [3]) and a_j pursues a *hegemonic* policy (axiom [4']). The theory is applicable if axioms (1), (2), (3) and (4') are simultaneously satisfied.

According to (4'), a_j prefers to ally with S_i or S_{-i} if $k_j \leqslant k(S_i) = k(S_{-i})$. If a_j allies with either S_i or S_{-i}, a_j becomes more powerful than one of the system's actors since a_j substitutes the power of the newly formed alliance for its own power in calculating its relative power position. However, since S_i and S_{-i} pursue equality policies, neither is willing to accept a_j as a member. All the axioms are satisfied and the theory is applicable.

Case 5. S_i pursues an *equality* policy, S_{-i} pursues a *hegemonic* policy and a_j pursues an *equality* policy. The theory is applicable if axioms (1), (2), (3), (3') and (4) are simultaneously satisfied when S_i acts in accordance with axiom (3), S_{-i} acts in accordance with axiom (3') and a_j acts in accordance with axiom (4). According to axiom (3'), S_{-i} prefers a_j to be an ally since D would increase in S_{-i}'s favor. However, by axiom (4), a_j does not prefer to join S_{-i} since $|D| = 0$ and u_j is maximized. There is no dominant actor in the system (axiom [1] is satisfied) and there is no actor opposing another by its power and hegemonic policy (axiom [2] is satisfied). The theory is applicable under this set of policy objectives since axioms (1), (2), (3), (3') and (4) are simultaneously satisfied.

Case 6. S_i, S_{-i} and a_j pursue *hegemonic* policies. The theory is applicable if axioms (1), (2), (3') and (4') are simultaneously satisfied with

97

S_i and S_{-i} act in accordance with axiom $(3')$ and a_j acts in accordance with axiom $(4')$.

The hegemonic policy of a_j (which is represented by axiom $[4']$) requires knowledge of the power relationships between a_j, S_i and S_{-i}. Since $k(S_i) = k(S_{-i})$, the following possibilities exist: $k_j < k(S_i)$, $k_j = k(S_i)$ and $k_j > k(S_i)$.

6a. $k_j < k(S_i) = k(S_{-i})$.

When $k_j < k(S_i)$, S_i and S_{-i} are more powerful than a_j. According to $(4')$, u_j increases if a_j increases its relative power position with respect to other actors in the system. In allying with either S_i or S_{-i}, a_j increases its relative power position over one actor in the system since a_j substitutes the power of the newly formed alliance for its own power in calculating its relative power position. According to $(3')$, S_i and S_{-i} are willing to admit a_j as a member of their respective alliances. Although we cannot determine which alliance a_j joins, the fact is that a_j allies with one of the opponents. *Axiom (1) is thereby violated* and the theory is inapplicable.

6b. $k_j = k(S_i) = k(S_{-i})$.

According to (i) of the axiom $(4')$, u_j increases if a_j allies with either S_i or S_{-i}. If a_j joins S_i (S_{-i}), a_j increases its relative power position with respect to S_{-i} (S_i). According to axiom $(3')$, S_i and S_{-i} are willing to admit a_j as a member to increase D in their favor. Although we cannot determine which alliance a_j joins, the fact is that a_j allies with one of the opponents. *Axiom (1) is not satisfied* and the theory is inapplicable.

6c. $k_j > k(S_i) = k(S_{-i})$.

According to $(4')$, a_j has no incentive to ally with either opponent since a_j by itself is more powerful than either S_i or S_{-i}. If this inequality holds, and all actors in the system pursue hegemonic policies, the *theory is applicable.*

To sum up, when S_i, S_{-i} and a_j pursue hegemonic policies, the theory is applicable only if $k_j > k(S_i) = k(S_{-i})$.

APPENDIX B
BALANCER VERSION, $k(S_i) > k(S_{-i})$

Case 2. a_j and S_{-i} pursue *equality policies* and S_i pursues a *policy of hegemony*. The theory is applicable if axioms (1), (2), (3), (3′) and (4) are simultaneously satisfied when a_j acts in accordance with axiom (4), S_i acts in accordance with axiom (3′) and S_{-i} acts in accordance with axiom (3).

2a. $k_j = D$

In this case a_j allies with S_{-i} and $|D| = 0$. $k(S_i) = k(S_{-i})a_j \epsilon S_{-i}$ and the *theory is applicable.*

2b. $k_j > D$

a_j seeks to minimize $|D|$ according to axiom (4). When the difference in power between S_i and S_{-i} decreases, the utility function of a_j increases. Thus if

2b.i. $k_j < 2D$

the utility functions of a_j and S_{-i} increase and a_j allies with S_{-i}. Now $k(S_{-i})a_j \epsilon S_{-i}$ is greater than $k(S_i)$ and *axiom (1) is not satisfied.*

On the other hand, if

2b.ii. $k_j \geqslant 2D$

a_j does not ally with S_{-i} since $|D|$ would increase as a result of such an alignment. *Axiom (2) is not satisfied* since $k(S_i) > k(S_{-i})$ and S_i pursues a policy of hegemony.

Case 3. S_i and a_j pursue *equality policies* and S_{-i} pursues a *policy of hegemony*. S_i and a_j act in accordance with axioms (3) and (4), respectively, and S_{-i} acts in accordance with axiom (3′). The theory is applicable if axioms (1), (2), (3), (3′) and (4) are mutually satisfied. (Note that this analysis is different from the analysis of case 2: in this case the *weaker* alliance pursues a policy of hegemony.)

3a. $D = k_j$

In this case a_j allies with S_{-i} and $|D| = 0$. S_{-i} seeks to increase D in its favor and is thus willing to admit a_j as a member since D will now be 0 (where previously $D > 0$). Consequently, $k(S_i) = k(S_{-i})_{a_j \epsilon S_{-i}}$ and the *theory is applicable.*

3b. $D < k_j$

Since S_{-i} pursues a policy of hegemony it will always be willing to admit a_j as a member to increase D in its favor. However, since a_j pursues a policy of equality, it will only ally with S_{-i} when

(i) $k_j < 2D$

When condition (i) holds, $|D|$ decreases and a_j's utility increases (axiom [4]). *Axiom (1) is not satisfied* as a result of a_j aligning with S_{-i} since there is now one actor in the system whose power is greater than that of the only other actor in the system (that is, S_i).

On the other hand, when

(ii) $k_j \geqslant 2D$

$|D|$ increases and a_j does not ally with S_{-i} (according to axiom [4]). Since S_i pursues an equality policy, axiom (2) is satisfied. There is no one actor whose power is greater than the total power of the remaining actors in the system and thus axiom (1) is satisfied. The *theory is applicable* in this case.

Case 4. S_i and S_{-i} pursue *policies of equality* (that is, they act in accordance with axiom [3]) and a_j pursues a *policy of hegemony* (that is, a_j acts in accordance with axiom [4']). The theory is applicable if axioms (1), (2), (3) and (4') are mutually satisfied.

The hegemonic policy of a_j (which is expressed by axiom [4']) requires knowledge of the power relationships between a_j, S_i and a_j, S_{-i}. Since $k(S_i) > k(S_{-i})$, the following possibilities exist: (a) when $k_j = D$, $k_j < k(S_i)$ and

$$k_j \underset{<}{\overset{>}{-}} k(S_{-i}),$$

and (b) when $k_j > D$,

$$k_j \underset{<}{\overset{>}{-}} k(S_i) \text{ and } k_j \underset{<}{\overset{>}{-}} k(S_{-i}).$$

4a. $D = k_j$. When $D = k_j$, $k_j < k(S_i)$ and $k_j \underset{<}{\overset{>}{-}} k(S_{-i})$.

4a.i. $k_j > k(S_{-i})$.

If a_j joins S_i it does not increase its relative power position with respect to S_{-i}. However if a_j allies with S_{-i}, S_i is no longer more powerful than a_j, $a_j \epsilon S_{-i}$. [When a_j joins S_{-i}, $k(S_i) = k(S_{-i})$]. According to axiom (4'), a_j has an incentive to join S_{-i}. S_{-i} admits a_j as a member since $|D|$ is equal to zero as a result and $u_{S_{-i}}$ is maximized according to axiom (3). The theory is applicable with $k(S_i) = k(S_{-i})_{a_j \epsilon S_{-i}}$.

4a.ii. $k_j \leqslant k(S_{-i})$.

According to (4′), a_j has an incentive to ally with S_i and S_{-i}. If a_j joins S_{-i}, it increases its relative power position with respect to S_i. When a_j is not a member of S_{-i}, $k_j < k(S_i)$. However when a_j is a member of S_{-i}, $k(S_i) = k(S_{-i})_{a_j \epsilon S_{-i}}$. On the other hand, if a_j joins S_i, a_j increases its relative power position with respect to S_{-i}. When a_j is not a member of S_i, $k_j \leqslant k(S_{-i})$. However, when a_j is a member of S_i, $k(S_i)_{a_j \epsilon S_i} > k(S_{-i})$. According to axiom (3), S_i is not willing to admit a_j as a member whereas S_{-i} is willing to admit a_j. Consequently, a_j joins S_{-i}. The theory is applicable and $k(S_i) = k(S_{-i})_{a_j \epsilon S_{-i}}$.

4b. $k_j > D$.

When $k_j > D$ it is possible that

$$k_j \gtrless k(S_i) \text{ and } k_j \gtrless k(S_{-i}).$$

4b.i. $k_j < k(S_i)$ and $k_j > k(S_{-i})$.

According to axiom (4′) a_j prefers to ally with S_{-i} thereby increasing its relative power position with respect to S_i. According to axiom (3), S_{-i} admits a_j as a member only when $k_j < 2D$ which is consistent with its policy objective of minimizing $|D|$. By admitting a_j as a member of S_{-i}, S_{-i} is now more powerful than S_i and *axiom (1) is not satisfied.*

On the other hand, if $k_j \geqslant 2D$, S_{-i} does not admit a_j as a member since in doing so, $|D|$ increases (which is inconsistent with the policy objective of S_{-i}). When $k_j \geqslant 2D$, there is no dominant actor in the system and axiom (1) is satisfied. Axiom (2) is also satisfied since there is no actor opposing another by its power *and* hegemonic policy. *All the axioms are simultaneously satisfied.*

4b.ii. $k_j = k(S_i)$ and $k_j > k(S_{-i})$.

a_j joins S_{-i} when $k_j < 2D$ for the reasons given in 4b.i above. *Axiom (1) is not satisfied* as a result.

When $k_j \geqslant 2D$, a_j does not ally with S_{-i} for the same reasons expressed in 4b.i. The *theory is applicable* in this case.

4b.iii. $k_j < k(S_{-i})$ and $k_j < k(S_{-i})$.

According to axiom (4′), a_j prefers to ally with either S_i or S_{-i}. If a_j allies with S_i, a_j increases its relative power position with respect to S_{-i} since $k(S_i)_{a_j \epsilon S_i} > k(S_{-i})$. On the other hand, if a_j allies with S_{-i}, a_j increases its relative power position with respect to S_i since $k(S_{-i})_{a_j \epsilon S_{-i}} > k(S_i)$. According to axiom (3), S_i is not willing to admit a_j as a member and S_{-i} admits a_j only when $k_j < 2D$. In admitting a_j to S_{-i}, *axiom (1) is not satisfied* since $k(S_{-i})_{a_j \epsilon S_{-i}} > k(S_i)$.

On the other hand, when $k_j \geqslant 2D$, S_{-i} does not admit a_j as a member (according to axiom [3]) and the *theory is applicable.*

4b.iv. $k_j < k(S_i)$ and $k_j = k(S_{-i})$.

According to axiom $(4')$, a_j prefers to ally with either S_i or S_{-i}. If a_j allies with S_i, $k(S_i)_{a_j \epsilon S_i} > k(S_{-i})$, whereas if a_j remains neutral, $k_j = k(S_{-i})$. On the other hand, if a_j allies with S_{-i}, $k(S_{-i})_{a_j \epsilon S_{-i}} > k(S_i)$, whereas if a_j remains neutral, $k_j < k(S_i)$. According to axiom (3), S_i is not willing to admit a_j as a member. S_{-i} admits a_j only when $k_j < 2D$ to decrease the difference in power between itself and S_i. When $k_j < 2D$, the theory is inapplicable. *Axiom (1) is not satisfied* since $k(S_{-i})_{a_j \epsilon S_{-i}} > k(S_i)$.

On the other hand, when $k_j \geqslant 2D$, S_{-i} does not admit a_j as a member (in accordance with its foreign policy objective of minimizing $|D|$) *and the theory is applicable.*

4b.v. $k_j > k(S_i) > k(S_{-i})$.

According to axiom $(4')$, a_j prefers to remain neutral in this case since a_j does not increase its relative power position by allying with either opponent. The theory is applicable.

Summing up case 4, when S_i and S_{-i} pursue equality policies, and the balancer nation, a_j, pursues a hegemonic policy, the theory is applicable if $D = k_j$ or if $k_j > D$ and $k_j \geqslant 2D$ or $k_j < 2D$ and $k_j > k(S_i)$.

Case 5. S_i and S_{-i} pursue *hegemonic policies* (in accordance with axiom $[3']$) and a_j pursues a *policy of equality* (in accordance with axiom $[4]$). The theory is applicable if axioms (1), (2), $(3')$ and (4) are simultaneously satisfied.

5a. $D = k_j$.

According to axiom (4), a_j seeks to minimize $|D|$ and consequently a_j allies with S_{-i}. According to axiom $(3')$, S_{-i} accepts a_j as a member since D changes in S_{-i}'s favor. The *theory is applicable* with $k(S_i) = k(S_{-i})_{a_j \epsilon S_{-i}}$.

5b. $k_j > D$.

According to axiom $(3')$, S_i and S_{-i} are willing to admit a_j. However, since a_j pursues an equality policy, a_j allies with S_{-i} only when $k_j < 2D$. In allying with S_{-i}, *axiom (1) is not satisfied* since $k(S_{-i})_{a_j \epsilon S_{-i}} > k(S_i)$.

On the other hand, when $k_j \geqslant 2D$, a_j does not ally with S_{-i}. *Axiom (2) is not satisfied* since $k(S_i) > k(S_{-i})$ and S_i pursues a policy of hegemony.

Case 6. S_i pursues an *equality policy* (in accordance with axiom $[3]$) while S_{-i} and a_j pursue *hegemonic policies* (in accordance with axioms $[3']$ and $[4']$, respectively). The theory is applicable if axioms (1), (2) (3), $(3')$ and $(4')$ are simultaneously satisfied.

6a. $D = k_j$.

Since a_j pursues a hegemonic policy, it is necessary to consider the following possibilities: $k_j > k(S_{-i})$, $k_j < k(S_{-i})$ and $k_j = k(S_{-i})$.

6a.i. $k_j > k(S_{-i})$.

According to axiom $(4')$, a_j prefers to ally with S_{-i} and in accordance with axiom $(3')$, S_{-i} will admit a_j. The *theory is applicable* and $k(S_i) = k(S_{-i})_{a_j \epsilon S_{-i}}$.

6a.ii. $k_j < k(S_{-i})$.

According to axiom $(4')$, a_j prefers to ally with S_{-i}, and according to $(3')$, S_{-i} is willing to admit a_j as a member. The *theory is applicable* and $k(S_i) = k(S_{-i})_{a_j \epsilon S_{-i}}$.

6a.iii. $k_j = k(S_{-i})$.

According to axiom $(4')$, a_j prefers to ally with S_{-i} and according to axiom $(3')$, S_{-i} is willing to admit a_j. The *theory is applicable* and $k(S_i) = k(S_{-i})_{a_j \epsilon S_{-i}}$.

6b. $k_j > D$.

Since a_j pursues a hegemonic policy, it is necessary to consider the following inequalities:

$$k_j \underset{<}{\overset{>}{-}} k(S_i) \text{ and } k_j \underset{<}{\overset{>}{-}} k(S_{-i}).$$

In all subcases of 6b, a_j allies with S_{-i} (according to axioms [4'] and [3'] except when $k_j > k(S_i) > k(S_{-i})$. When $a_j \epsilon S_{-i}$, $k(S_{-i}) > k(S_i)$ and *axiom (1) is not satisfied*. The theory is applicable only when $k_j > k(S_i) > k(S_{-i})$.

Summing up, when a_j and S_{-i} pursue hegemonic policies and S_i pursues an equality policy, the theory is applicable when $k_j = D$ or $k_j > k(S_i) > k(S_{-i})$.

Case 7. S_i and a_j pursue *hegemonic policies* (in accordance with axioms [3'] and [4'], respectively), while S_{-i} pursues a *policy of equality* (in accordance with axiom [3]). The theory is applicable if axioms $(1), (2), (3), (3')$ and $(4')$ are simultaneously satisfied.

This analysis differs from the analysis in case 6 in that the *stronger alliance* pursues a policy of hegemony in this case.

7a. $D = k_j$.

Since a_j pursues a hegemonic policy, it is necessary to consider the following possibilities: $k_j > k(S_{-i})$, $k_j = k(S_{-i})$ and $k_j < k(S_{-i})$.

7a.i. $k_j > k(S_{-i})$.

In this case a_j does not have any incentive to join S_i because its ability to increase its relative power position with respect to S_{-i} does not occur as a result of such an alignment. On the other hand, if a_j joins S_{-i}, a_j is in a better power position with respect to S_i. Because S_{-i} seeks to minimize $|D|$ (according to its policy objective of equality), S_{-i} admits a_j. The theory is applicable with $k(S_i) = k(S_{-i})_{a_j \epsilon S_{-i}}$.

7a.ii. $k_j = k(S_{-i})$.

In accordance with axiom $(4')$, a_j is willing to ally with either S_i or S_{-i}. If a_j allies with S_i, a_j increases its relative power position with respect to S_{-i}. On the other hand, if a_j allies with S_{-i}, a_j is no longer in a weaker power position with respect to S_i. According to axiom (3), S_{-i} admits a_j in order to minimize $|D|$. By axiom $(3')$, S_i accepts a_j as a member in order to increase D in S_i's favor. Although we cannot determine which alliance a_j joins, we do know that a_j prefers joining an alliance rather than remaining neutral. If a_j joins S_i, *axioms (1) and (2) are not satisfied.* On the other hand, if a_j joins S_{-i}, the *theory is applicable.*

7a.iii. $k_j < k(S_{-i})$.

As in 7a.ii, *axioms (1) and (2) may not be satisfied.* For reasons similar to those discussed in 7a.ii, above, a_j may ally with either S_i or S_{-i}.

7b. $k_j > D$.

Since a_j pursues a hegemonic policy, it is necessary to consider the following possibilities:

$$k_j \overset{<}{\underset{>}{-}} k(S_i) \text{ and } k_j \overset{<}{\underset{>}{-}} k(S_{-i}).$$

7b.i. $k_j < k(S_i)$ and $k_j > k(S_{-i})$.

According to $(4')$, a_j has no incentive to ally with S_i but if a_j allies with S_{-i}, a_j increases its power position with respect to S_i. According to axiom (3), S_{-i} admits a_j as a member when $k_j < 2D$. If $k_j < 2D$, a_j joins S_{-i} and *axiom (1) is not satisfied.*

On the other hand, if $k_j \geqslant 2D$, S_{-i} does not admit a_j as a member, since in doing so $|D|$ increases (contrary to the policy objective pursued by S_{-i}). Hence, when $k_j \geqslant 2D$, *axiom (2) is not satisfied* since S_i is more powerful than S_{-i} and S_i pursues a hegemonic policy.

7b.ii. $k_j = k(S_i)$ and $k_j > k(S_{-i})$.

The analysis is the same here as in 7b.i above. When $k_j < 2D$, *axiom (1) is not satisfied* and when $k_j \geqslant 2D$, *axiom (2) is not satisfied.*

7b.iii. $k_j < k(S_i)$ and $k_j < k(S_{-i})$.

In accordance with axiom $(4')$, a_j prefers to ally with either S_i or S_{-i} rather than remain neutral. If $k_j \geqslant 2D$, a_j joins S_i since S_{-i} does not admit a_j (according to axiom [3]). Axioms (1) and (2) are not satisfied as a result of a_j aligning with S_i. On the other hand, if $k_j < 2D$, we cannot determine which alliance a_j joins. If a_j joins S_{-i}, *axiom (1) is not satisfied.* If a_j joins S_i, *axioms (1) and (2) are not satisfied.*

7b.iv. $k_j < k(S_i)$ and $k_j = k(S_{-i})$.

The analysis in this case is the same as in 7b.iii above. If $k_j \geqslant 2D$, a_j joins S_i since S_{-i} is not willing to admit a_j (in accordance with S_{-i}'s policy objective of equality). *Axioms (1) and (2) are not satisfied* in this case. On the other hand, if $k_j < 2D$, a_j joins either S_i or S_{-i}. If a_j joins S_i, *axioms (1) and (2) are not satisfied*. If a_j joins S_{-i}, *axiom (1) is not satisfied*.

7b.v. $k_j > k(S_i) > k(S_{-i})$.

In this case a_j have no incentive to ally with either opponent. *Axiom (2) is thereby not satisfied* since S_i is more powerful than S_{-i} and S_i pursues a hegemonic policy.

Summing up, when the more powerful alliance, S_i, and the balancer nation, a_j, pursue hegemonic policies, and the weaker alliance, S_{-i}, pursues an equality policy, the theory is applicable only when $D = k$ and $k_j > k(S_{-i})$. The theory may be applicable if a_j joins S_{-i} when $D = k_j$ and $k_j \leqslant k(S_{-i})$.

Case 8. S_i, S_{-i} and a_j pursue hegemonic policies. S_i and S_{-i} act in accordance with axiom $(3')$ and a_j acts in accordance with axiom $(4')$. The theory is applicable if axioms (1), (2), $(3')$ and $(4')$ are simultaneously satisfied.

8a. $D = k_j$.

Since a_j pursues a hegemonic policy, it is necessary to consider the following possibilities in determining a_j's behavior: $k_j > k(S_{-i})$, $k_j = k(S_{-i})$ and $k_j < k(S_{-i})$.

8a.i. $k_j > k(S_{-i})$.

In this case a_j has an incentive to join S_{-i} and increase its relative power position with respect to S_i. Since S_{-i} wants to change D to its favor, S_{-i} is willing to admit a_j as a member. According to axiom $(4')$, a_j has no incentive to ally with S_i since a_j cannot increase its relative power position with respect to S_{-i}. Consequently, a_j joins S_{-i} and the *theory is applicable* with $k(S_i) = k(S_{-i})_{a_j \epsilon S_{-i}}$.

8a.ii. $k_j < k(S_{-i})$.

In this case, a_j allies with either opponent since u_j increases in both cases (according to axiom $[4']$). According to axiom $(5')$, both S_i and S_{-i} are willing to admit a_j as a member. If a_j allies with S_{-i}, the *theory is applicable* with $k(S_i) = k(S_{-i})_{a_j \epsilon S_{-i}}$. On the other hand, if a_j chooses to align with S_i, *axioms (1) and (2) are not satisfied*.

8a.iii. $k_j = k(S_{-i})$.

Again as in 8a.ii above, a_j has an incentive to ally with either opponent. If a_j joins S_{-i}, the *theory is applicable*. On the other hand, if a_j joins S_i, *axioms (1) and (2) are not satisfied*.

8b. $k_j > D$.

Since a_j pursues a hegemonic policy, it is necessary to consider the following possibilities in determining a_j's behavior:

$$k_j \underset{<}{\overset{>}{-}} k(S_i) \text{ and } k_j \underset{<}{\overset{>}{-}} k(S_{-i}).$$

8b.i. $k_j < k(S_i)$ and $k_j > k(S_{-i})$.

According to axiom $(4')$, a_j joins S_{-i}, thereby increasing its relative power position with respect to S_i. *Axiom (1) is not satisfied* as a result of such an alignment since $k(S_{-i})_{a_j \epsilon S_{-i}} > k(S_i)$.

8b.ii. $k_j < k(S_i)$ and $k_j < k(S_{-i})$.

According to axioms $(4')$ and $(3')$, a_j joins either S_i or S_{-i}. If a_j joins S_{-i}, *axiom (1) is not satisfied*. On the other hand, if a_j joins S_i, *axioms (1) and (2) are not satisfied*.

8b.iii. $k_j = k(S_i)$ and $k_j > k(S_{-i})$.

According to axiom $(4')$, a_j joins S_{-i} in order to increase its relative power position with respect to S_i. In accordance with axiom $(3')$, S_{-i} admits a_j as a member. *Axiom (1) is not satisfied* because $k(S_{-i})_{a_j \epsilon S_{-i}} > k(S_i)$.

8b.iv. $k_j < k(S_i)$ and $k_j = k(S_{-i})$.

According to axioms $(4')$ and $(3')$, a_j joins either S_i or S_{-i}. If a_j joins S_{-i}, *axiom (1) is not satisfied*. On the other hand, if a_j joins S_i, *axioms (1) and (2) are not satisfied*.

8b.v. $k_j > k(S_i) > k(S_{-i})$.

According to axiom $(4')$, a_j has no incentive to ally with either opponent. *Axiom (2) is not satisfied* as a result since $k(S_i) > k(S_{-i})$ and S_i pursues a hegemonic policy.

Summing up case 8, if S_i, S_{-i} and a_j pursue hegemonic policies, the balancer version of the theory is applicable only when $D = k_j$ and $k_j > k(S_{-i})$. The theory may be applicable when $D = k_j$ and $k_j \leqslant k(S_{-i})$ if a_j joins S_{-i}.

APPENDIX C
CONSISTENCY, SOUNDNESS AND APPLICABILITY WHEN INITIAL POWER DISTRIBUTION AMONG NATIONS IS EQUAL

THREE-NATION SYSTEM

In a three-nation system, we must consider the following situations: (1) no nation pursues a hegemonic policy; (2) one nation pursues a hegemonic policy; (3) two nations pursue hegemonic policies and (4) three nations pursue hegemonic policies.

In the first situation, only one case must be examined since there are no opposing actors in the system. However, six cases must be considered when one nation in the system pursues a hegemonic policy. Either a_1, a_2, or a_3 may pursue hegemonic policies. Furthermore, if a_1 (a_2 or a_3) pursues a hegemonic policy, a_1 may oppose a_2 (a_1 or a_3) or a_3 (a_1 or a_2). If two nations in the system pursue hegemonic policies, twelve cases must be examined. Either a_1 and a_2, a_2 and a_3, a_1 and a_3 pursue hegemonic policies while a_3, a_1, a_2 pursue equality policies, respectively. If, for example, a_1 and a_2 pursue hegemonic policies, a_1 may oppose a_2 or a_3, or a_2 may oppose a_1 or a_3. Four cases must therefore be examined when a_1 and a_2 pursue hegemonic policies ([1] a_1 opposes a_2; [2] a_1 opposes a_3; [3] a_2 opposes a_1; [4] a_2 opposes a_3). Similarly, four cases must be examined when a_2 and a_3 pursue hegemonic policies, and when a_1 and a_3 pursue hegemonic policies. Finally, six cases must be examined when all nations in the system pursue hegemonic policies: a_1 may oppose a_2 or a_3; a_2 may oppose a_1 or a_3; and a_3 may oppose a_1 or a_2. Thus, a total of twenty-five cases must be examined in a three-nation system. (From now on, an equality policy will be represented by E, and a hegemonic policy by H.)

Case 1: a_1, a_2, and a_3 pursue E.

All nations act in accordance with axiom (4). Since no nation opposes any other nation, there are no alliances in the system and axioms (1), (2) and (4) are satisfied.

107

Cases 2 - 7: The mutual satisfiability of axioms (1), (2), (4), (3) and (3′) is examined when one nation acts in accordance with axiom (3′), one nation acts in accordance with axiom (4), and one nation acts in accordance with axiom (3). In cases 2 and 3, a_2 acts in accordance with axiom (3′) and a_3, a_1 act in accordance with axioms (4), (3), respectively. (That is, a_2, a_1 are opposing nations in case 2 and a_2, a_3 are the opposing nations in case 3). Similarly, a_3 (a_1) acts in accordance with axiom (3′) in cases 4 and 5, and 6 and 7). Since the reasoning is similar for cases 2 - 7, only the analysis of case 2 is given.

Case 2: a_1 pursues E, a_2 pursues H and a_3 pursues E. a_2 opposes a_1 (axiom [3′]) but, since a_3 pursues an equality policy (in accordance with axiom [4]), a_3 does not ally with a_2. Axioms (1), (2), (3), (4) and (3′) are satisfied and the theory is applicable.

Cases 8 - 19: The mutual satisfiability of axioms (1), (2), (3), (3′), (4) and (4′) is examined when two nations pursue hegemonic policies and one nation pursues an equality policy. Twelve cases are generated: there are three orderings of two H's and one E (EHH, HEH and HHE), and for each ordering four cases must be considered. The reasoning is identical for each ordering, so only cases 8 - 11 are described.

Case 8: a_1 pursues E, a_2 pursues H and a_3 pursues H. a_3 opposes a_2; a_1 does not ally with either a_2 or a_3, and the theory is applicable.

Case 9: a_1 pursues E, a_2 pursues H and a_3 pursues H. a_3 opposes a_1. In this case, a_2 allies with a_3 (according to axiom [4′]) and axiom (1) is violated. The theory is inapplicable.

Case 10: a_1 pursues E, a_2 pursues H and a_3 pursues H. a_2 opposes a_3; a_1 does not ally with either a_2 or a_3, and the theory is applicable.

Case 11: a_1 pursues E, a_2 pursues H and a_3 pursues H. a_2 opposes a_1; a_3 allies with a_2 (according to axiom [4′]), and axiom (1) is violated. The theory is inapplicable.

Cases 20 - 25: In cases 20 - 25, two nations act in accordance with axiom (3′) and one nation acts in accordance with axiom (4′). In cases 20 and 21, a_1 opposes a_2 and a_3, respectively; a_1 and a_2 (a_1 and a_3) act in accordance with axiom (3′) and a_3 (a_2) adopts the policy objective in axiom (4′) in cases 20 and 21. a_2 opposes a_1 and a_3, respectively, for cases 22 and 23, and a_3 opposes a_1 and a_2, respectively, for cases 24 and 25. Since the analysis is identical for these six cases, only the analysis of case 20 is presented.

Case 20: a_1 pursues H, a_2 pursues H and a_3 pursues H. a_1 opposes a_2; a_1 and a_2 act in accordance with axiom (3′), and a_3 acts in accordance with axiom (4′). According to axiom (4′), a_3 prefers to ally with a_1 or a_2 rather than remain neutral. Axiom (1) is not satisfied and as a result, the theory is inapplicable, given this set of policy objectives in a three-nation system.

In sum, we analyzed twenty-five cases that could occur in a three-nation system. We had to consider six cases when two nations pursued equality policies; twelve cases when two nations pursued hegemonic policies; and six cases when all nations pursued hegemonic policies. We found the balance of power to be applicable when:

all nations pursued E	(1) case
two nations pursued E	(6) cases
two nations pursued H	(6) cases

Hence, the theory was found to be applicable in 13 cases for a three-nation system. We found the balance of power theory to be inapplicable when:

two nations pursued H	(6) cases
all nations pursued H	(6) cases

The theory was found to be inapplicable in 12 cases for a three-nation system.

FOUR-NATION SYSTEM

The mutual satisfiability of axioms (1), (2), (3), (3'), (4) and (4') are examined when: four nations pursue E policies, one nation pursues an H policy, two nations pursue H policies, three nations pursue H policies, and four nations pursue H policies. If one nation, say a_1, pursues an H policy, its opponent may be a_2, a_3, or a_4. Thus there are twelve cases to consider when one nation pursues an H policy, since a_2, a_3 or a_4 may also pursue H policies, and their opponents may be any one of the remaining nations in the system. When two nations in the system pursue hegemonic policies, thirty-six cases must be examined; all possible orderings of two H's and two E's are examined in determining the mutual satisfiability of axioms (1), (2), (3), (3'), (4) and (4'). Similarly, if three nations pursue hegemonic policies, thirty-six cases must be considered. Finally, twelve cases must be examined when four nations in the system pursue hegemonic policies.

Case 1: a_1, a_2, a_3, a_4 pursue E.

No nation opposes any other nation; there are no alliances and the theory is applicable.

Cases 2 – 13: Three nations pursue E, and one nation pursues H. Twelve cases must be examined if it is possible for any nation to pursue H and oppose any other nation in the system. The mutual satisfiability of axioms (1), (2), (3), (4) and (3') are examined in twelve cases. The reasoning is similar for all these cases, and so only case 2 is detailed:

109

Case 2: EEEH

a_4 opposes a_3 : there are no alliances and the theory is applicable.

Cases 14 – 49: If two nations in the system pursue hegemonic policies, thirty-six cases must be considered in examining the mutual satisfiability of axioms (1), (2), (3), (3′), (4), and (4′). Six cases must be considered for each ordering of two H's and two E's. Further, there are six possible orderings of two H's and two E's (EEHH, EHEH, HEEH, HHEE, HEHE, EHHE). Since the reasoning is similar for each ordering of two E's and two H's, only the analysis of one such ordering is presented.

Cases 14 – 19: EEHH

14: a_4 opposes a_3 ; there are no alliances and the theory is applicable.

15: a_1 opposes a_2 ; a_3 allies with a_4 (according to axiom [4′]); a_1 allies with a_2 (according to axiom [4]); the theory is applicable.

16: a_4 opposes a_1 ; a_3 allies with a_4 and a_2 then allies with a_1. The theory is applicable.

17: a_3 opposes a_4 ; analysis is the same as in case 14.

18: a_3 opposes a_2 ; analysis is the same as in case 15.

19: a_3 opposes a_1 ; analysis is the same as in case 16.

Cases 50 – 85: In these cases the mutual satisfiability of axioms (1), (2), (3), (3′), (4) and (4′) is examined when three nations in the system pursue hegemonic policies and one nation pursues an equality policy. There are four orderings of three H's and one E (EHHH, HEHH, HHEH, HHHE). Furthermore, for each ordering of three H's and one E, nine cases must be considered: any nation that pursues a hegemonic policy may oppose any other nation in the system. Consequently, a total of thirty-six cases must be examined (9 x 4). Since the reasoning is identical for each ordering of three H's and one E, only the analysis of cases 50 – 58 is given.

Cases 50 – 58: EHHH

50: a_4 opposes a_3 ; a_2 joins a_3 or a_4. As a result, a preponderance exists, with either a_2 and a_4 more powerful than a_3, or a_2 and a_3 more powerful than a_4. According to axiom (4), a_1 allies with the weaker side. The theory is applicable.

51: a_4 opposes a_2. Same analysis as in case 50.

52: a_4 opposes a_1. a_1 does not accept a_3 or a_2 as an ally (according to axiom [3′]); if both a_2 and a_3 ally with a_4, the theory is inapplicable. If only a_2 allies with a_4 at first, a_3 still prefers to join a_2 and a_4 rather than ally with a_1 (a_1 would now accept a_3 as an ally). The theory is inapplicable in this case.

53 – 55: a_3 opposes a_4, a_2 and a_1, respectively. The analyses are the same as in cases 50 – 52 and the theory is inapplicable in the case when a_3 opposes a_1.

110

56 – 58: a_2 opposes a_1, a_3 and a_4, respectively. The analyses are the same as in cases 50 – 52 and the theory is inapplicable in the case when a_2 opposes a_1.

Cases 86 – 97: Although there is only one ordering of four nations pursuing hegemonic policies, twelve cases must be examined to determine the satisfiability of axioms (1), (2), (3') and (4').

Any nation with a hegemonic policy may oppose any other nation in the system. Since there are four nations in the system, there are three possible opponents for each nation, and so a total of twelve (4 x 3) cases must be examined.

Cases 86 – 97: HHHH

86: a_4 opposes a_3; a_1 joins a_4 or a_3; a_2 prefers to ally with the more powerful side. The theory is inapplicable.

87 – 88: a_4 opposes a_2 and a_1, respectively. The theory is inapplicable in both cases, due to the sequencing of events outlined in case 86, above.

89 – 97: are similar cases, for nations a_3, a_2, and a_1, respectively, acting as the hegemonic initiator; the theory is inapplicable in all these cases.

In sum, we had to analyze ninety-seven cases for a four-nation system. There were twelve cases to consider when three nations pursued equality policies; thirty-six cases to consider when two nations pursued equality policies and two nations pursued hegemonic policies; thirty-six cases to consider when three nations pursued hegemonic policies; and twelve cases to consider when all nations pursued hegemonic policies.

We found the balance of power theory to be applicable when:

all nations pursued E	(1) case
two nations pursued E	(36) cases
three nations pursued H	(24) cases
three nations pursued E	(12) cases

The theory was applicable in seventy-three cases.

We found the balance of power theory to be inapplicable when:

three nations pursued H	(12) cases
all nations pursued H	(12) cases

The theory was inapplicable, then, in twenty-four cases.

FIVE-NATION SYSTEM

The mutual satisfiability of axioms (1), (2), (3), (3'), (4) and (4') is examined in a five-nation system when: (a) all nations pursue E; (b) one nation pursues H; (c) two nations pursue H; (d) three nations pursue H; (e) four nations pursue H; and (f) five nations pursue H. If one nation, for example a_1, pursues a hegemonic policy, it can potentially oppose a_2, a_3, a_4 or a_5.

Therefore, we must consider twenty cases when one nation pursues an H policy, since any nation in the system can pursue an H policy, and their opponents may be any one of the remaining nations in the system. When two nations in the system pursue H policies, a total of eighty cases must be considered; one hundred-twenty cases must be considered when three nations pursue hegemonic policies; eighty cases must be considered when four nations pursue hegemonic policies; and, finally, twenty cases must be considered when all nations pursue hegemonic policies.

Case 1: EEEEE

The theory is applicable in this case, as no nation opposes any other nation and no alliances are formed.

Cases 2 – 21: EEEEH, EEEHE, EEHEE, EHEEE, HEEEE

There are four cases for each ordering of E's and H's. All of these cases satisfy axioms (1) – (4') simultaneously.

Cases 22– 101: These cases involve all orderings of two H's and three E's. There are ten such orderings. In each ordering, there are eight cases to consider. Cases 22 – 101 satisfy axioms (1), (2), (3), (3'), (4) and (4') simultaneously. Here is an example of an analysis of one ordering (EEEHH):

Cases 22 – 29:

22: a_5 opposes a_4; there are no alliances and the theory is applicable.

23: a_5 opposes a_3; a_4 allies with a_5; a_1 or a_2 then allies with a_3 and one remains neutral. The theory is applicable.

24 – 25: the analysis of these cases will be identical to the analysis of 23, with a_3 being replaced by a_2 and a_1, respectively.

26 – 29: these cases are identical to the analyses of cases 22 – 25, with a_4 replacing a_5 in each case.

Cases 102 – 221: These cases involve all orderings of three H's and two E's; there are ten such orderings. In each ordering there are twelve cases to consider; six cases imply that the theory is applicable and six cases imply that the theory is inapplicable, in each ordering. Consequently, there is a total of sixty possible cases in which the theory is applicable and sixty cases in which the theory is inapplicable. Here is an example of an analysis of one ordering.

Cases 102 – 113: EEHHH

102: a_5 opposes a_4; a_3 allies with either a_4 or a_5; a preponderance results; a_1 or a_2 joins the weaker side and the theory is applicable.

103: the analysis is the same as in case 102, with a_3 replacing a_4.

104: a_5 opposes a_2; a_3 or a_4 allies with a_5; a_1 then allies with a_2. a_1 and a_2 will not admit a_3 (if it has not already allied with a_5). a_3 prefers to ally with a_4 and a_5 rather than remain neutral. a_4 and a_5 accept a_3 as a member. The theory is therefore inapplicable.

105: the analysis is the same as in case 104 with a_1 replacing a_2. The theory is inapplicable.

106 - 109: the analyses of these cases are identical to the analyses of cases 102 - 105, with a_4 replacing a_5. For half of the cases the theory is applicable, but the theory is inapplicable in the remaining half. (That is, in two cases the axioms are satisfied and in two cases the axioms are not satisfied.)

110 - 113: the analyses of these cases are identical to the analysis of 102 - 105, with a_3 replacing a_5.

As this example indicates, it is necessary to consider twelve cases for each ordering ot three H's and two E's. Six cases satisfy the theory's axioms and six cases do not satisfy the theory's axioms.

Cases 222 - 301: These cases involve all orderings of four H's and one E. There are five such orderings, and sixteen cases to consider in each ordering. None of these cases satisfy the theory's axioms; consequently, there is a total of eighty inapplicable cases for these orderings. Here is an example of the analysis of one ordering.

Cases 222 - 237: EHHHH

222: a_5 opposes a_4; a_3 joins a_4 or a_5; a_1 joins the weaker side (according to axiom [4]); a_2 prefers to ally with either side rather than remain neutral. a_4 and a_5 are willing to admit a_3 as a member. The theory is therefore inapplicable.

223: a_5 opposes a_3; a_4 joins a_3 or a_5; a_2 prefers to join the more powerful side. a_1 allies with the weaker side but axiom (1) is violated, and the theory is inapplicable.

224: a_5 opposes a_2; the case proceeds as above, and the theory is inapplicable.

225: a_5 opposes a_1. a_2 allies with a_5 according to axiom (4'). a_3 and a_4 both prefer to ally with the stronger side. Axioms (1) and (2) are violated and the theory is inapplicable.

226 - 229: a_4 opposes every other nation in the system; the analysis proceeds as in 222 - 225 above.

230 - 233: a_3 opposes every other nation in the system; the analysis proceeds as in 222 - 225 above.

234 - 237: a_2 opposes every other nation in the system; the analysis proceeds as in 222 - 225 above.

As this example indicates, it is necessary to consider sixteen cases for each ordering of four H's and one E. None of these cases simultaneously satisfy axioms (1), (2), (3), (3'), (4) and (4').

Cases 302 - 321: There are twenty cases to consider when five nations pursue hegemonic policies. There are four cases to consider when a_5

opposes a_1, a_2, a_3 and a_4, respectively; four cases when a_4 opposes every other nation, and so on. All twenty cases imply that four nations oppose the remaining nation. (See the analysis of four nations pursuing hegemonic policies.) Axioms (1) and (2) are violated in all cases where the ordering is HHHHH.

In sum, then, we had to analyze 321 cases for a 5-nation system. There were 20 cases to consider when 4 nations pursued equality policies; 80 cases to consider when 3 nations pursued equality policies; 120 cases to consider when 3 nations pursued hegemonic policies; 80 cases to consider when 4 nations pursued hegemonic policies; and 20 cases to consider when all nations pursued hegemonic policies.

The balance of power theory was applicable when:

all nations pursued E	(1) case
two nations pursued E	(60) cases
three nations pursued E	(80) cases
four nations pursued E	(20) cases

The theory was found to be applicable in 161 cases. The theory was inapplicable when:

three nations pursued H	(60) cases
four nations pursued H	(80) cases
all nations pursued H	(20) cases

In a 5-nation system, then, the theory was found to be inapplicable in 160 cases.

SIX-NATION SYSTEM

The mutual satisfiability of axioms (1) - (4') is examined when 1, 2, 3, 4, 5 and 6 nations pursue H policies. A total of 961 cases must be examined in determining the theory's applicability: one case when 6 nations pursue E policies; 30 cases when one nation pursues an H policy; 150 cases when 2 nations pursue H policies; 300 cases when 3 nations pursue H policies; 300 cases when 4 nations pursue H policies; 150 cases when 5 nations pursue H policies; and 30 cases when 6 nations pursue H policies.

(1) *All nations pursue E.* There is only one case to consider here. The theory is applicable in this case.

(2) *Five nations pursue E and one nation pursues H.* There are six orderings for these policies, and five cases to consider in each ordering. The theory is applicable in each case. Consequently, the theory is applicable for thirty cases, since axioms (1), (2), (3), (3'), (4) and (4') are simultaneously satisfied.

114

(3) *Four nations pursue E and two nations pursue H.* There are fifteen orderings for these policies, and ten cases to consider in each ordering. As a result, there is a total of 150 cases to consider and the theory is applicable in each case.

(4) *Three nations pursue E and three nations pursue H.* There are twenty orderings of these policies, and fifteen cases to consider in each ordering. There is a total of 300 cases to consider and the theory is applicable in each case.

(5) *Four nations pursue H and two nations pursue E.* There are fifteen orderings of these policies, and twenty cases to consider for each ordering. In each ordering, twelve cases satisfy axioms (1), (2), (3), (3'), (4) and (4'), while eight cases do not simultaneously satisfy these axioms. (Whenever one of the nations pursuing an equality policy is opposed, the theory is inapplicable. On the other hand, if a nation pursuing a hegemonic policy is opposed, the theory is applicable because the nations pursuing equality policies ally with the weaker side.) Consequently, there is a total of 180 cases in which the theory is applicable (15 x 12) and 120 cases in which the theory is not applicable (15 x 8).

(6) *Five nations pursue H and one nation pursues E.* There are six orderings of these policies, and twenty-five cases to consider for each ordering. There is a total of 150 cases, and the theory is inapplicable in each case.

(7) *All nations pursue H.* There is one ordering when all nations pursue H and there are thirty cases to consider (every nation opposes five others). The theory is inapplicable in all thirty cases.

In sum, we had to consider 961 cases for a 6-nation system. There were 30 cases to consider when 5 nations pursued equality policies; 150 cases to consider when 4 nations pursued equality policies; 300 cases to consider when 3 nations pursued equality policies; 300 cases to consider when 4 nations pursued hegemonic policies; 150 cases to consider when 5 nations pursued hegemonic policies; and 30 cases to consider when all nations pursued hegemonic policies.

The theory was applicable when:

all nations pursued E	(1) case
five nations pursued E	(30) cases
four nations pursued E	(150) cases
three nations pursued E	(300) cases
two nations pursued E	(180) cases

The theory was applicable, then, in 661 cases.

The theory was inapplicable when:

all nations pursued H	(30) cases
five nations pursued H	(150) cases
four nations pursued H	(120) cases

The theory was found to be inapplicable in 300 cases.

REFERENCES

REFERENCES

Aron, Raymond. 1960. The Quest for a Philosophy of Foreign Affairs. In *Contemporary Theory in International Relations*, ed. S. Hoffman, pp. 79-91. Englewood Cliffs: Prentice Hall.

——————. 1966. *Peace and War*. Garden City: Doubleday.

Bertrand, Pierre. 1889. ed., *Lettres Inedites de Talleyrand a Napeoleon, 1800-1809*. Paris: s.n.

Butterfield, Herbert. 1953. *Christianity, Diplomacy and War*. New York: Abingdon-Cokesbury.

——————. 1966. The Balance of Power. In *Diplomatic Investigations*, eds. H. Butterfield and M. Wight. pp. 143-48. Cambridge: Harvard Univ. Press.

Caplow, Theodore. 1956. A Theory of Coalitions in the Triad. *American Sociological Review* 21:489-93.

Chatterjee, Partha. 1972. The Classical Balance of Power Theory. *Journal of Peace Research* 9:51-61.

Chertkoff, Jerome M. 1967. A Revision of Caplow's Coalition Theory. *Journal of Experimental Psychology* 3:172-77.

——————. 1970. Sociopsychological Theories and Research on Coalition Formation. In *The Study of Coalition Behavior*, eds. E. W. Kelley and M. Lierserson. pp. 320-22. New York: Holt, Rinehart & Winston.

Churchill, Winston. 1948. *The Second World War: The Gathering Storm*. Boston: Houghton-Mifflin.

Claude, Inis L., Jr. 1967. *Power and International Relations*. New York: Random House.

Cobden, Richard. 1867. *Political Writings, I*. London: s.n.

——————. 1956. In *The Anglo-American Tradition in Foreign Affairs*, eds. A. Wolfers and L. W. Martin. p. 203. New Haven: Yale Univ. Press.

Collier, David, and Messick, Richard. 1975, Prerequisites Versus Diffusion: Testing Alternative Models of Social Security Adoption. *American Political Science Review* 69:1299-1315.

119

Fay, Sidney B. 1937. Balance of Power. *Encyclopedia of the Social Sciences* 2:395-99.

Gamson, William A. 1961. A Theory of Coalition Formation. *American Sociological Review* 26:373-82.

Gooch, G. P. 1939. European Diplomacy Before the War in the Light of the Archives. *International Affairs* 18.

Gulick, Edward. 1955. *Europe's Classical Balance of Power.* New York: Cornell Univ. Press.

Haas, Ernst B. 1953a. The Balance of Power as a Guide to Policy-Making. *Journal of Politics* 15:370-98.

――――――. 1953b. The Balance of Power: Prescription, Concept or Propaganda? *World Politics* 5:442-77.

Hassell, Arthur. 1914. *The Balance of Power, 1715-1789.* New York: Macmillan.

Healy, B., and Stein, A. 1971. The Balance of Power in International History. *Journal of Conflict Resolution* 17:33-61.

Herz, John H. 1959. *International Politics in the Atomic Age.* New York: Columbia Univ. Press.

Hoffman, Stanley. 1972. Weighing the Balance of Power. *Foreign Affairs* 50:618-43.

Jessup, Phillip, ed. 1935. *Neutrality: Its History, Economics and Law.* New York: Columbia Univ. Press.

Kaeber, E. 1906. "Die Idee dis Europaischen Gleichgeivichts" in der publizistischen Literatur, vom. 16, bis Zur Mitte des 18. Jahrhunderts, Berlin, pages 22-25.

Kaplan, Morton. 1957a. Balance of Power, Bipolarity and other Models. *American Political Science Review* 51:3.

――――――. 1957b. *System and Process in International Relations.* New York: Wiley.

――――――. 1969. Variants on Six Models of the International System. In *International Politics and Foreign Policy*, ed. J. Rosenau. pp. 291-303. New York: Free Press.

Kaplan, Morton; Burns, Arthur Lee; Quandt, Richard E. 1960. Theoretical Analysis of the "Balance of Power." *Behavioral Science* 5:24-252.

Kissinger, Henry. 1957. *A World Restored.* Boston: Houghton-Mifflin.

Kulski, Wladyslaw W. 1964. *International Politics in the Revolutionary Age.* Philadelphia: Lippincott.

Lerche, Charles O. 1956. *Principles of International Politics.* New York: Oxford Univ. Press.

Liska, George. 1957. *The International Equilibrium.* Cambridge: Harvard Univ. Press.

Machiavelli, Niccolo. n.d. *Il Principe* (Burd, ed.). Chapter 20.

Morgan, Patrick. 1977. *Theories and Approaches to International Politics*. New Brunswick: Transaction Books.

Morgenthau, Hans. 1951. *In Defense of the National Interest*. New York: Knopf.

_____. 1956. The Essays on Counsels, Civil and Moral. In *The Anglo-American Tradition in Foreign Affairs*, eds. A. Wolfers and L. W. Martin. New Haven: Yale Univ. Press.

_____. 1973. *Politics Among Nations*. New York: Knopf.

Nicholson, Harold. 1946. *The Congress of Vienna*. New York: Harcourt, Brace.

_____. 1960. Perspective on Peace: A Discourse. In *Perspective on Peace, 1910-1960*. New York: Praeger.

Organski, A.F.K. 1958. *World Politics*. New York: Knopf.

Ostrom, Charles. 1977. Evaluating Alternative Foreign Policy Decision Making Models: An Empirical Test Between an Arms Race Model and an Organization Model. *Journal of Conflict Resolution* 21:235-66.

Ostrom, Charles, and Aldrich, John H. 1978. The Relationship Between Size and Stability in the Major Power International System. *American Journal of Political Science* 22:743-71.

Overbury, Sir Thomas. 1903. In *Observations in His Travels in Stuart Tracts: 1603-1693*, ed. C. H. Firth. p. 227. Constable.

Penrose, E. F. 1965. *The Revolution in International Politics*. London: Frank Cass.

Pollard, A. F. 1923. The Balance of Power. *Journal of the British Institute of International Affairs* 2:53-64.

Riker, William. 1962. *The Theory of Political Coalitions*. New Haven: Yale Univ. Press.

Rippy, J. F. 1938. *America and the Strife of Europe*. Chicago: Univ. of Chicago Press.

Rosecrance, Richard N. 1963. *Action and Reaction in World Politics*. Boston: Little Brown.

Schleicher, Charles. 1954. *Introduction to International Politics*. New York: Prentice Hall.

Schwarzenberger, Georg. 1941. *Power Politics*. London: Jonathan Cape Ltd.

Singer, J. David; Bremer, Stuart; Stuckey, John. 1972. Capability Distribution, Uncertainty, and Major Power War, 1870-1965. In *Peace, War and Numbers*, ed. B. M. Russett. pp. 19-48. Beverly Hills: Sage.

Spykman, Nicholas J. 1942. *America's Strategy in World Politics*. New York: Harcourt, Brace.

Sweet, Paul. 1941. *Frederich Von Gentz: Defender of the Old Order*. Madison: Univ. of Wisconsin Press.

Taylor, A.J.P. 1954. *The Struggle for Mastery in Europe, 1848-1918.* Oxford: Clarendon Press.

de Vattel, Emmerich. 1916. *The Law of Nations.* Washington, D.C.: s.n.

von Gentz, Frederick. 1941. In *Frederich Von Gentz: Defender of the Old Order,* ed. P. Sweet. Madison: Univ. of Wisconsin Press.

Waltz, Kenneth. 1964. The Stability of a Bipolar World. *Daedalus* 93: 881-909.

——————. 1967. International Structure, National Force, and the Balance of World Power. *Journal of International Affairs* 21:215-31.

Wight, Martin. 1966. Balance of Power. In *Diplomatic Investigations,* eds. H. Butterfield and M. Wight. pp. 149-75. London: Allen and Unwin.

Wilder, Raymond. 1952. *The Foundations of Mathematics.* New York: Wiley & Sons.

Wolfers, Arnold. 1962. *Discord and Collaboration.* Baltimore: Johns Hopkins Press.

Wright, Quincy. 1942. *A Study of War.* Chicago: Univ. of Chicago Press.

Yalem, Ronald. 1972. Tripolarity and the International System. *Orbis* 15:1051-63.

Zinnes, Dina. 1967. An Analytical Study of the Balance of Power Theories. *Journal of Peace Research* 4:270-88.

——————. 1970. Coalition Theories and the Balance of Power. In *The Study of Coalition Behavior,* eds. E. W. Kelley and M. Leiserson. pp. 336-68. New York: Holt, Rinehart & Winston.

Manuscript Submission and Previous Publications

MANUSCRIPT SUBMISSION

The *Monograph Series in World Affairs,* published quarterly since 1963 by the Graduate School of International Studies, focuses on theoretic developments and research results dealing with contemporary problems of international relations. In treatment and scope, scholarly pieces that fall between journal and book length manuscripts are suitable. Thoughtful, relevant studies presented analytically in historical and social science frameworks are welcome. Statements of fact or opinion remain the responsibility of the authors alone and do not imply endorsement by the editors or publishers.

Submission: Send manuscripts in triplicate to Karen A. Feste, Editor, Monograph Series in World Affairs, Graduate School of International Studies, University of Denver, Denver, Colorado 80208. Manuscripts already published, scheduled for publication elsewhere, or simultaneously submitted to another journal are not acceptable. Manuscripts will be returned to authors only if accompanied, on submission, by a stamped, self-addressed envelope.

Abstract: Each manuscript must be summarized with a one to two page abstract indicating framework, setting, methodology, and findings.

Author Identification: On a separate page, specify manuscript title, full name and address of author(s), academic or other professional affiliations, and indicate to whom correspondence and galley proofs should be sent. A brief paragraph describing the author's research interest and recent publications should accompany the manuscript. Since manuscripts are sent out anonymously for evaluation, the author's name and affiliation should appear only on a separate covering sheet, as should all footnotes identifying the author.

Form: Manuscripts should be typed double-spaced (including footnotes), with footnotes, references, tables, charts, and figures on separate pages. Authors should follow the Chicago *Manual of Style* except as noted below regarding references. Footnotes should be numbered by chapter. Excessive footnoting should be avoided. Tables, figures, and charts should be mentioned in the text, numbered with Arabic numerals, and given a brief, descriptive title. A guideline should be inserted to indicate their appropriate place in the text.

References: In the text: All source references are to be identified at the appropriate point in the text by the last name of the author, year of publication, and pagination where needed. Identify subsequent citations of the same source in the same way as the first, not using *ibid., op. cit.,* or *loc. sit.* Examples: If author's name is in the text, follow it with year in parentheses [...Morcan, (1969)...]. If author's name is not in the text, insert, in parentheses, the last name and year, separated by a comma [...(Davidson, 1957)...]. Pagination follows year of publication after a colon [...(Budd, 1967:24)...]. Give both last names for dual authors; for more than two, use *et al.* If there is more than one reference to one author and year, distinguish them by letters added to the year [...(1977a)...].

In the Reference Section: The reference section must include all references cited in the text. The use of *et al.* is not acceptable; list the full name of all authors. The format for books: author, year of publication, title, place of publication, publisher. The format for journals: author, year of publication, title of article, name of periodical, volume, number, month, page.

Evaluations: Each manuscript is reviewed by the editor and at least two other readers. Almost always, two reviews are sought outside the University of Denver. General policy is to complete the evaluation process and communicate the editorial decision to the author within four months. Full referee reports are sent to the author. Anonymity of author and reviewer is preserved. Scholars who have furnished reviews of manuscripts during the year will be listed in the final issue of each volume.

Accepted Manuscripts: Manuscripts accepted for publication are subject to copy editing in our office. Edited versions (and later, page proofs) will be sent to the author for approval before materials are given to the printer. These must be returned within ten days. Due to prohibitive cost, substantial changes proposed at the page proof stage will be made at the discretion of the editors; or, alternatively, the cost of such changes will be billed to the author. Instructions for the preparation of camera-ready artwork will be forwarded to the author upon acceptance of the manuscript for publication. This artwork (tables, graphs, figures, photos) must be completed and approved before the production process will be initiated. Ten copies of the published monograph will be supplied free of charge to the senior author.

Permission Policy: To obtain permission to photocopy or to translate materials from the *Monograph Series,* please contact the editor.

Advertising: Current rates and specifications may be obtained by writing the managing editor.

Rates: *Individuals:* single issue, $5.00 plus $1.50 postage and handling; annual subscription, $14.00. *Libraries and Institutions:* annual subscription, $18.00; single issue, $5.00 plus postage and handling. Back issues available at $3.00 per single issue.

MONOGRAPH SERIES IN WORLD AFFAIRS
Previous Publications

Volume 1, 1963-1964 Series

Rupert Emerson. *Political Modernization: The Single-Party System.*

Wendell Bell and Ivar Oxall. *Decisions of Nationhood: Political and Social Development in the British Caribbean.*

Volume 2, 1964-1965 Series

John C. Campbell. *The Middle East in the Muted Cold War.*

Dean G. Pruitt. *Problem Solving in the Department of State.*

James R. Scarritt. *Political Change in a Traditional African Clan: A Structural-Functional Analysis of the Nsits of Nigeria.*

Volume 3, 1965-1966 Series

Jack Citrin. *United Nations Peacekeeping Activities: A Case Study in Organizational Task Expansion.*

Ernst B. Haas and Philippe C. Schmitter. *The Politics of Economics in Latin American Regionalism: The Latin American Free Trade Association after Four Years of Operation* (out of print).

Taylor Cole. *The Canadian Bureaucracy and Federalism, 1947-1965.*

Arnold Rivkin. *Africa and the European Common Market: A Perspective.* (Revised Second Edition)

Volume 4, 1966-1967 Series

Edwin C. Hoyt. *National Policy and International Law: Case Studies from American Canal Policy.*

Bruce M. Russett and Carolyn C. Cooper. *Arms Control in Europe: Proposals and Political Constraints.*

Vincent Davis. *The Politics of Innovation: Patterns in Navy Cases.*

Yaroslav Bilinsky. *Changes in the Central Committee Communist Party of the Soviet Union, 1961-1966.*

Volume 5, 1967-1968 Series

Ernst B. Haas. *Collective Security and the Future International System.*

M. Donald Hancock. *Sweden: A Multiparty System in Transition?*

W.A.E. Skurnik, Editor, Rene Lemarchand, Kenneth W. Grundy and Charles F. Andrain. *African Political Thought: Lumumba, Nkrumah, and Toure.*

Volume 6, 1968-1969 Series

Frederick H. Gareau. *The Cold War 1947-1967: A Quantitative Study.*

Henderson B. Braddick. *Germany, Czechoslovakia, and the "Grand Alliance" in the May Crisis, 1938.*

Robert L. Friedheim. *Understanding the Debate on Ocean Resources.*

Richard L. Siegel. *Evaluating the Results of Foreign Policy: Soviet and American Efforts in India.*

Volume 7, 1969-1970 Series

Quincy Wright. *On Predicting International Relations, The Year 2000.*

James N. Rosenau. *Race in International Politics: A Dialogue in Five Parts.*

William S. Tuohy and Barry Ames. *Mexican University Students in Politics: Rebels without Allies?*

Karl H. Hoerning. *Secondary Modernization: Societal Changes of Newly Developing Nations—A Theoretical Essay in Comparative Sociology.*

Volume 8, 1970-1971 Series

Young W. Kihl. *Conflict Issues and International Civil Aviation: Three Cases* (out of print).

Morton Schwartz. *The "Motive Forces" of Soviet Foreign Poicy, A Reappraisal.*

Joseph I. Coffey. *Deterrence in the 1970s* (out of print).

Edward Miles. *International Administration of Space Exploration and Exploitation.*

Volume 9, 1971-1972 Series

Edwin G. Corr. *The Political Process in Colombia.*

Shelton L. Williams. *Nuclear Nonproliferation in International Politics: The Japanese Case.*

Sue Ellen M. Charlton. *The French Left and European Integration.*

Volume 10, 1972-1973 Series

Robert W. Dean. *Nationalism and Political Change in Eastern Europe: The Slovak Question and the Czechoslovak Reform Movement.*

M. Donald Hancock. *The Bundeswehr and the National People's Army: A Comparative Study of German Civil-Military Polity.*

Louis Rene Beres. *The Management of World Power: A Theoretical Analysis.*

George A. Kourvetaris and Betty A. Dobratz. *Social Origins and Political Orientations of Officer Corps in a World Perspective.*

Volume 11, 1973-1974 Series

Waltraud Q. Morales. *Social Revolution: Theory and Historical Application.*

David O'Shea. *Education, the Social System, and Development.*

Robert H. Bates. *Patterns of Uneven Development: Causes and Consequences in Zambia.*

Robert L. Peterson. *Career Motivations of Administrators and Their Impact in the European Community.*

Volume 12, 1974-1975 Series

Craig Liske and Barry Rundquist. *The Politics of Weapons Procurement: The Role of Congress.*

Barry M. Schutz and Douglas Scott. *Natives and Settlers: A Comparative Analysis of the Politics of Opposition and Mobilization in Northern Ireland and Rhodesia.*

Vincent B. Khapoya. *The Politics of Decision: A Comparative Study of African Policy Toward the Liberation Movements.*

Louis Rene Beres. *Transforming World Politics: The National Roots of World Peace.*

Volume 13, 1975-1976 Series

Wayne S. Vucinich. *A Study in Social Survival: Katun in the Bileca Rudine.*

Jan F. Triska and Paul M. Johnson. *Political Development and Political Change in Eastern Europe: A Comparative Study.*

Louis L. Ortmayer. *Conflict, Compromise, and Conciliation: West German-Polish Normalization 1966-1976.*

James B. Bruce. *Politics of Soviet Policy Formation: Khrushchev's Innovative Policies in Education and Agriculture.*

Volume 14, 1976-1977 Series

Daniel J. O'Neil. *Three Perennial Themes of Anti-Colonialism: The Irish Case.*

Thomas Lobe. *United States National Security Policy and Aid to the Thailand Police.*

David F. Cusack. *Revolution and Reaction: The Internal and International Dynamics of Conflict and Confrontation in Chile.*

David F. Cusack. *The Death of Democracy and Revolution in Chile, 1970-1973.* Slide Show-Narrative Cassette (out of print).

Robert E. Harkavy. *Spectre of a Middle Eastern Holocaust: The Strategic and Diplomatic Implications of the Israeli Nuclear Weapons Program.*

Volume 15, 1977-1978 Series

Lewis W. Snider. *Arabesque: Untangling the Patterns of Conventional Arms Supply to Israel and the Arab States and the Implications for United States Policy on Supply of "Lethal" Weapons to Egypt.*

Bennett Ramberg. *The Seabed Arms Control Negotiations: A Study of Multilateral Arms Control Conference Diplomacy.*

Todd M. Sandler, William Loehr, and Jon T. Cauley. *The Political Economy of Public Goods and International Cooperation.*

Ronald M. Grant and E. Spencer Wellhofer, Editors. *Ethno-Nationalism, Multinational Corporations, and the Modern State.*

Volume 16, 1978-1979 Series

Sophia Peterson. *Sino-Soviet-American Relations: Conflict, Communication and Mutual Threat.*

Robert H. Donaldson. *The Soviet-Indian Alignment: Quest for Influence.*

Volume 17, 1979-1980 Series

Pat McGowan and Helen E. Purkitt. *Demystifying "National Character" in Black Africa: A Comparative Study of Culture and Foreign Policy Behavior.*

Theodore H. Cohn. *Canadian Food Aid: Domestic and Foreign Policy Implications.*

Robert A. Hoover. *Arms Control: The Interwar Naval Limitation Agreements.*

Lisa Robock Shaffer and Stephen M. Shaffer. *The Politics of International Cooperation: A Comparison of U.S. Experience in Space and in Security.*

Volume 18, 1980-1981 Series

Massiye Edwin Koloko. *The Manpower Approach to Planning: Theoretical Issues and Evidence from Zambia.*

Harry Eckstein. *The Natural History of Congruence Theory.*

P. Terrence Hopmann, Dina A. Zinnes, and J. David Singer. *Cumulation in International Relations Research.*

Philip A. Schrodt. *Preserving Arms Distributions in a Multi-Polar World: A Mathematical Study.*

Volume 19, 1981-1982 Series

Michael D. Ward. *Research Gaps in Alliance Dynamics.*

Theresa C. Smith. *Trojan Peace: Some Deterrence Propositions Tested.*

Roslyn L. Simowitz. *The Logical Consistency and Soundness of the Balance of Power Theory.*

Book format and printing
by
DEPARTMENT OF GRAPHICS
University of Denver